EVERY WOMAN CAN

The Conroy Method to Safety, Security & Self-Defense

MARY CONROY, Ed. D.
Professor
Department of Physical Education
California State University, Los Angeles

EDWARD RITVO, M.D.
Professor
Division of Child Psychiatry and Mental Retardation
School of Medicine
University of California, Los Angeles

Photography by Julie Hadden

D1198214

Grosset & Dunlap
Publishers New York

We wish to express our appreciation to
Francesca Quon for her adroit typing and Julie
Hadden, our photographer, whose skills made
us—deep friends—appear as villainous attackers
and ferocious defenders.

This book is dedicated to
ROMA CONROY
and
the memory of
our beloved parents
MAURICE R. CONROY, Ph.D.
FRANCES DAVIS RITVO
and
MAX RITVO, M.D.

Contents

Preface   XV

1. **The Common Sense of Self-defense**   1
   - If It's You—It's 100 Percent   1
   - Don't Be Tomorrow's Headline   2
   - Things Your Mother Never Told You   3
   - The Proof of the Pudding   5
   - When and When Not to Use Physical Defense   6
   - Your Legal Responsibility   7
   - Strategy Versus Tactics   8

2. **Strategies for Self-defense**   9
   - Eliminate Potential Dangers   10
   - Recognize and Avoid Dangers   11
   - Tactics to Avoid Fighting   14
   - Fight When Necessary   16
   - Planning Your Attack   16
   - Delivering Your Attack   20
   - Summary   21

3. **The Golden Rules of Personal Safety**   23
   - Precautions in the Home   23
   - Install Safety Devices   23
   - Proper door and window locks   23
   - Electronic warning system   26
   - Through-the-door viewer   26
   - Properly Dispose of Keys and Valuables   28
   - Keys   28
   - Cash   28
   - Important papers   28
   - Know Your Baby-sitter   29
   - Discourage Break-ins   29
   - Cooperate with a Burglar   30
   - Inform Police of Suspicious Entries   30
   - Prepare for a Leave or Vacation   31
   - Stop deliveries   31
   - Notify the police   31

Order vacation phone service   31
Have yard work attended to   32
Use an on-off lighting device   32
Let a neighbor know   32
Form a neighborhood watch   32
Phone Precautions   32
Prepare for emergencies   32
Ward off obscene callers   33
Protect your privacy   33
Elevator Advice   34
Car Cautions   34
Public Transportation   37
Airplanes   37
Trains, buses, and subways   37
Taxis   37
Traveling Tips   38
Planning Your Trip   38
Packing   38
Transportation   38
Identifying Luggage   38
Meeting Strangers   39
Your Hotel   39
Leave Itinerary in Case of Emergency   39
Public Area Precautions   40
Walk the Streets with Caution   40
Avoid Isolation   41
Evade Exhibitionists   41
Watch Your Purse   42
Summary   42

4. Tactics for Defense   45
Mental Preparedness   45
Your Seven Tactics   46
Screams   47
Thumb Gouge   48
Groin Pull   53
Finger Jab   56
Knee Lift   57

Double-Hand Blow 59
Kicks 59
Front Kick 61
Side Kick 63
Rear Kick 63
Knee Break 64
The Conroy Method 64
Maneuvers 65
Single-Wrist Maneuver 66
Double-Wrist Maneuver 66
Front-Choke Maneuver 68
Rear-Choke Maneuver 69
Hair Maneuver 71
Ground Maneuver 72
Unconventional Maneuvers 72
Double-Knee Drop 74
Summary 76

5. **Weapons** 77
Weapons for Defense 79
Noisemaker 80
Purse 81
Book or Package 81
Newspaper or Magazine 82
Flashlight 82
Keys 82
Umbrella, Broomstick, or Mop Handle 83
Pen or Pencil 84
Purse Contents 85
Tear Gas 85
Commercially Available Self-defense Items 85
Defense Against an Assailant's Weapons 86
Defense Against a Knife Attack 86
Gun Attack 89
Bludgeon Attack 91
Summary 92

6. Fourteen Dangerous Situations   **93**
   Bunco   93
   Dating Dangers   95
      How Not to Meet Men   95
      Four Commonsense Rules for Dating   96
      How to Handle an Overzealous Date   96
   Vicious Dog   97
   Gang of Small Children   98
   Woman Beating   98
   Violent Women   101
   Burglary   102
   Forceful Intruder   105
   Threat of Being Bound by an Assailant   106
   Robbery   106
   Two or More Assailants   109
   Aggravated Assault   110
   Murder   111
   Rape-Murder   112
   Summary   117

7. Protecting Children from Sexual
   Offenders   **119**
   An Introduction   119
   Parents' Responsibility   120
      Eliminating Danger   120
      Recognizing and Avoiding Danger   121
   Children's Responsibility   121
      Eliminating Danger   121
      Recognizing and Avoiding Danger   122
      Fighting   123
   Incest   123
   Minimizing Psychological Damages Caused
      by Sexual Abuse   124
   Reporting Child Molestations to the Police   125

8. Rape—Don't Take It Lying Down   **127**
   Historical Background   128
   Misconceptions About Rape   129

Psychology of the Rapist   131
The Psychotic   132
The Pervert   132
The Opportunist   133
Strategies for Dealing with Rape   134
Anatomy of a Rape   139
Stage 1: Rapist Selects Victim   139
Stage 2: Rapist Contacts Victim   139
Stage 3: Rapist Gains Control of Victim   139
Stage 4: Physical Assault   139
Stage 5: Postrape   139
What to Do If Raped   140
Observe and Recall Details   140
Immediately Notify the Police   140
Call a Friend   140
Cooperate with Police Questioning   140
Undergo Medical Examination   141
Report to the Police Station   141
Take Legal Action   142
Postrape Reactions   142
A True Experience   144
A Success Story   147

9. **Help the Police to Help You**   **149**
Describing the Assailant   149
Taking Postattack Action   151
Summary   152

10. **Shaping Up for Self-defense**   **155**
Specific Exercises   156
Physical Aids to Learning   167
With a Little Help from Your Friends   171
Mental Aids to Learning   172

11. **Twenty Days to a More Powerful and
Secure You**   **173**
Daily Lesson Plans   173
Test Your Knowledge   186

Self-defense Resource List   **191**
Index   **195**

Figures

Figure Number	Topic	Page(s)
2–1	Run, Scream, and Prepare to Fight	14-15
2–2	Your Five Weapons	17
2–3	Your Four Targets	19
3–1	Types of Locks	24-25
4–1	Thumb Gouge	49
4–2	Thumb Gouge with Glasses	50
4–3	Thumb Gouge from Strangulation with Object—Supine Position	50
4–4	Thumb Gouge from Strangulation with Object	51
4–5	Eye Gouge from Rear	52
4–6	Thumb Gouge Against Suffocation Attack	53
4–7	Groin Pull	54
4–8	Finger Jab	56
4–9	Finger Jab from Lying Position	56
4–10	Knee Lift	58
4–11	Double-Hand Blow	58
4–12	Length of Legs	60
4–13	Incorrect Kicks	60
4–14	Front Kick	62
4–15	Side Kick	62
4–16	Rear Kick	62
4–17	Knee Break	65
4–18	Single-Wrist Maneuver	66
4–19	Double-Wrist Maneuver	67
4–20	Front-Choke Maneuver; Tactic 1: Bent-Arm Choke	68
4–21	Front-Choke Maneuver; Tactic 2: Straight-Arm Choke	69
4–22	Rear-Choke Maneuver	70-71
4–23	Hair Maneuver	71-72
4–24	Ground Maneuver; Tactic 1: Sitting-	73-74

Position Release

4–25   Ground Maneuver; Tactic 2: Lying-
        Position Release   75
4–26   Double-Knee Drop
5–1   Using a Purse as a Weapon   76
5–2   Using a Newspaper as a Weapon   81
5–3   Using Keys as a Weapon   82
5–4   Using a Broom as a Weapon   83
5–5   Using a Pencil as a Weapon   83
5–6   Defense Against a Knife   84
5–7   Rape Defense Against a Knife   87
5–8   Defense Against a Gun   88
5–9   Defense Against a Bludgeon   90
6–1   Defense Against a Woman   91
6–2   Defense Against a Forceful Intruder   102
6–3   Defense Against a Robber   105
6–4   Defense Against Two or More   108-109
        Assailants   110
8–1   Defense Against a Rapist
9–1   Describing the Assailant   137-38
10–1   Head Rolls   151
10–2   Arm Circles   156
10–3   Push-ups   157
10–4   Straddle Stretches   158
10–5   Legs Over   159
10–6   Sit-ups   160
10–7   Kneeling Stretches   161
10–8   Cross-Leg Stretches   162
10–9   Knee Squats   163
10–10   Jump Kicks   163
10–11   Leg Raises   164
10–12   Arm Drops   165
10–13   Side Bends   165
10–14   Using a Ball for Practicing the Thumb   166
        Gouge   167
10–15   Using Rolled Mats for Practicing Kicks   168
10–16   Using a Pillow for Practicing the
        Thumb Gouge   169

10–17   Using a Pillow for Practicing the Finger
          Jab   169
10–18   Using a Pillow for Practicing the Groin
          Pull   169
10–19   Using a Pillow for Practicing the
          Double-Hand Blow   170
10–20   Using a Pillow for Practicing the Knee
          in the Groin   170

PREFACE

Dear Reader:

Congratulations! By picking up this book you have just taken a positive action that could save your life. Congratulations are in order because you have selected and opened a book on a frightening problem. How can you, as a woman, deal with your escalating risk of becoming a statistic as the victim of a violent attack or a sexual assault? That is the subject of this book.

Our fifteen years of research and experience have proved that psychological evasion or denial lies behind the failure of most women to deal with danger realistically. If our cover and title caught your eye, you are among a fortunate minority of women who can face the existence of this threat. Unfortunately, most women are still psychologically paralyzed by the prospect of violence. The sad fact is that the most popular "self-defense technique" is denial. We deny the thought of terrifying topics—we avoid thinking about the threat of nuclear war—because we are convinced that there is no realistic action we can take to ensure our safety. This book is designed to reassure and convince you that simple, effective action *can* be taken by you. We offer a step-by-step approach to developing the knowledge necessary to live safely. You will learn precautionary and life-saving skills. When you have completed our book, you will have the confidence to act on this knowledge and to use these skills.

Be assured from the beginning that we will not be dealing with such preconceived notions of self-defense as judo, karate, kung fu, or aikido, represented by Hollywood stereotypes. (Keep your black belt for your basic black dress.)

The Conroy Method of Self-defense is *not* a martial art. Women involved in the program have been surprised and pleased to discover that technical skills, years of study, continual practice, and great physical strength are not required. The Conroy Method is specifically designed to be easily mastered by all women—young or old, agile or clumsy, tall or small, weak or strong. The basic, simple skills acquired in the Conroy Method are learned in several hours and have proved to be more effective than the techniques taught in the more exotic martial arts. We also do not suggest that you place your confidence in handguns, purse weapons, or chemical devices such as tear gas. These weapons can be lost, forgotten, or used against you. Each of them requires that you place your confidence in something other than yourself. When you master the skills outlined in our program, you will have at your disposal the ultimate weapon for your defense—YOUR OWN BODY.

Good   luck!

Mary Conroy
Edward Ritvo

EVERY WOMAN CAN

The Conroy Method to Safety, Security & Self-Defense

Chapter 1
The Common Sense
of Self-defense

If It's You—It's 100 Percent

IT can happen to you. IT may happen to you—and it is best to anticipate that IT will happen to you. That is the best way to be prepared for IT and to react properly if IT does happen to you.

What is IT? IT is a man leaping into your car, thrusting a knife to your throat, and telling you to drive to the desert. IT is a hard tug on your purse in a crowded street. IT is a repairman in your home suddenly turning on you and saying, "Into the bedroom and strip off your clothes." IT is a "nice" date who suddenly pushes you down and clutches at your skirt. IT is the thousands of attacks on women taking place every hour, every day, every night—the ones occurring even now, as you read these words, and making tomorrow's headlines. IT is the fear, the harm, the lifelong emotional scars suffered by unprepared women at the hands of brutal attackers.

How many attacks occur on women each minute, each day, each week? FBI Uniform Crime Report statistics show us that in the past ten years rape has increased by 83 percent, aggravated assault by 68 percent, burglary by 51 percent, robbery by 42 percent, and murder by 28 percent; but as you know, these statistics don't tell even a part of the story. Most attacks are never reported, since many victims don't want "the hassle of publicity." If a woman is not seriously injured or if her theft is minor, she may well say, "I just want to forget the whole thing." Many other attacks are only belatedly reported. For example, a recent Los Angeles newspaper had this glaring headline: "Wilshire Rapist Attacks Third Victim in Week." The ensuing story told how a rapist, "about 5'8" tall and having a thin build, attacked a 27-year-old model four nights ago on Wilshire Boulevard." The woman told the police that she was late in reporting the incident because she had been "sick and embarrassed."

Because of such factors, most attacks never make tomorrow's head-lines; thus statistics are inaccurate. Even if the statistics were accurate, would it help you to know that, according to a recent FBI Crime Report, one burglary takes place every 10 seconds, one larceny-theft every 5 sec-onds, one robbery every 78 seconds, one aggravated assault every 60 sec-onds, one forcible rape every 8 minutes, and one murder every 27 minutes in the United States? No, these figures would not motivate you to learn psychological preparedness for safety or self-defense techniques. The only statistic that really means something to you is—100 percent. If you, your mother, sister, or girl friend is attacked—then it's 100 percent.

Don't Be Tomorrow's Headline

No "logical" woman would argue with the fact that dangers do exist in her daily life, and if she is to be mentally and physically prepared for them, she must:

1. Eliminate dangerous situations by proper planning.
2. Recognize and avoid danger by being alert.
3. Fight vigorously when serious danger strikes, thus minimizing the possibility of being killed, physically injured, or psychologically scared.

In view of such obvious facts, why do women today do so little to protect themselves properly? Are they being illogical? Yes! (Men too! We don't mean to exclude them.) To prove this point, the most common rea-son given by women for not learning self-defense is that they don't have the necessary physical abilities and strength. This is obviously an irra-tional answer because the first two principles of self-defense listed above involve no physical strength or skill whatsoever. The third principle, fight vigorously, does require some skill. However, as we shall show, the degree of skill needed is not difficult to acquire.

The real reason that most women fail to learn self-defense tech-niques lies in the psychological area. You, like all human beings, simply do not like to think about situations that make you uncomfortable or anxious, such as the possibility of being attacked. One of the purposes of this book will be to explore some of these psychological factors. Remember the scary shadows on the ceiling that frightened you at night when you were six years old? They always disappeared when mother left the hall light on. So too will your fears of being attacked disappear in the light of reason. Take, for instance, the irrational notion just mentioned about the need to be strong to successfully protect yourself. Most women believe that great physical strength is necessary to break away from a burly assailant. As we will show, the Conroy Method of Self-defense can be easily mastered by any woman who has sufficient coordination and strength to get herself out of bed in the morning and hook up her bra strap. Such really complex tasks as putting on eye makeup or driving a car require far more coordination than it takes to fight a would-be assailant.

Psychological preparedness is not easily mastered. As we examine some of the factors that lead to psychological resistance, it will become clear that you will have to face thoughts that are scary. They may be so frightening, in fact, that you'll have nightmares. There could also be embarrassing reactions from those close to you. One woman who read our book had her feelings hurt by a roommate who called her a "paranoid nut" when she put new locks on their apartment doors. She profited more than her embarrassment cost. Let us remind you of an old saying: "Anything of value has its price as well as its rewards." The price we ask you to pay will be to expend some mental effort, to take some simple precautions, and to learn some simple skills. This effort will be amply repaid by increased feelings of self-confidence and the knowledge that you are not likely to become tomorrow's headline.

Things Your Mother Never Told You

Chances are your mother never read a book like this! In fact, only a short while ago, the things that are discussed in this book weren't talked about in polite society and at home and were rarely even whispered about among friends. The words *assault* and *rape* were taboo. The mere notion of being prepared for such events by thinking about them ahead of time was also taboo. Only a "bad girl" would ask questions about such subjects.

The "don't talk about it, don't think about it" attitude, which a "proper girl" was supposed to have, led to two negative consequences. First, it left her totally unprepared for the realities of life. Second, and just as dangerously, it laid the foundation for the poisonous suspicion that still exists today—namely, if a woman is raped, she must have been "asking for it" or she "deserved it."

These two false legacies, which are unfortunately still widespread, will be challenged in this book. Regarding the first, you will find that the darkness of ignorance is best dispelled by the light of knowledge. In our book, you will learn and thus gain self-confidence. Regarding the second, we wish to protect you from the unnecessary guilt that has ruined the lives of women who have been assaulted and raped. The poisonous prejudices of our Victorian heritage must be shed like leaves in late autumn. We are a new generation; we can benefit from new knowledge.

The Victorian attitude of avoiding unpleasant topics relevant to self-defense and the sad implication of compliance, which still hounds women who have been raped, do not exist by chance. As with all general attitudes within a society, they have unconscious psychological roots and superficial justifications. The deep roots are a need to avoid anxiety and feelings of panic. The best way, for example, to avoid feeling anxious about nuclear warfare destroying all of us is to never think about World War III. The best way to avoid the fear that arises if you imagine yourself as a victim of rape is to never think about it. This may seem like a strange place to mention the Boy Scout's motto, but because women were never Boy Scouts, we shall: It is "Be prepared." To be prepared means to think ahead through situations that have not yet occurred. To do this you must be able to tolerate the anxiety that accompanies imagining fearful and dangerous situations.

Thus, we can see reasons why self-defense for women has only recently become popular. It takes courage for you to realize that "It can happen to you" and to think of frightening situations that may give you nightmares. In addition, your friends may ridicule you, and your family may believe you are wasting your time and your energy.

It takes courage for you to ignore your friends' ridicule and to tolerate the anxiety that naturally accompanies learning self-defense. Yet, once you have finished this book, you will be better prepared to live safely in our dangerous society, and your courage and efforts will be amply rewarded.

When you started this book, you were probably unaware that your emotions would become involved. You thought that your attention would be focused on the skills and techniques to be learned. Indeed, when we began teaching self-defense, we had a similar focus. Much to our surprise, one of our first students, who had been doing very well in the first three sessions, appeared after class and requested a private conference. She confessed that she had developed fears of walking from the bus stop to her apartment. We thought that she was unusually sensitive. After discussing her fears, she was able to proceed with the course. During the next semester, several more women also "confessed" their preoccupation with fears of being attacked. We became curious and interviewed other students. We found that many had similar fearful reactions. Typically, at about the second or third session, the women became aware of the dangers about them and of their vulnerability. One put it graphically, "I feel like I've just learned that I'm lost in a dangerous jungle with lions and tigers. I've been given a gun with only one bullet—so I'm scared."

Further analysis revealed that our initial attempts to motivate women by emphasizing the first two strategies of self-defense—namely, eliminate dangers and recognize and avoid danger—were backfiring. They produced anxieties on a subconscious level by bringing into consciousness previously repressed fears of dangers. This recognition of potential danger is a necessary step in learning. In other words, don't be put off by anxiety. Feelings that you are being followed, nightmares of being attacked, or sudden suspicions when in familiar surroundings are normal. In fact, such feelings mean that you are really immersing yourself in the subject. These suspicions will work to your advantage. They will abate as your self-defense skills develop and as your confidence grows.

A typical example of increasing self-confidence was given by one of our readers. Initially, upon studying the book, she had a nightmare in which she was attacked by two men and awoke screaming. After completing the book and learning the skills, she reported having had the same dream. But this time she successfully defended herself and woke up feeling secure.

At the expense of being redundant, let us repeat: (1) Expect to become paranoid. (2) Expect moments of anxiety when in previously comfortable situations. (3) Expect people to tease you about studying self-defense. (4) Expect to have regrets about studying self-defense. (5) Expect these feelings to subside and to feel more self-assured and secure as your skills and knowledge increase.

The Proof of the Pudding

We don't simply expect you to believe us when we say that what you will gain from this book will more than outweigh any discomfort it may engender. The following two stories, which were found in a local newspaper this week, will offer the proof of the pudding that we are going to bake together.

The headline read TWO WOMEN REPEL RAPE ATTEMPTS. The first story told of a twenty-one-year-old Vietnamese woman who was walking to the bus at 7:30 A.M. when she was attacked by a man who struck her in the face and dragged her to the ground. As he was pulling at her clothing she got one foot free and kicked him in the groin. Her screams attracted the attention of a citizen who called the police. The assailant was arrested moments later on suspicion of attempted rape.

In the second case, a thirty-two-year-old woman was emptying trash in the rear of her apartment building when she was grabbed by a six-foot 200-pound man. As he ripped at her blouse, she kneed him in the groin. The man staggered off in pain.

When our mothers were young, these stories would never have been written.Women weren't taught to defend themselves because women weren't supposed to defend themselves. Fortunately, today the situation is reversed. Women have gained the right to live as equals in the real world. These rights bring obligations, one of which is to learn the skills necessary to be safe and comfortable in this new world. You'll be surprised at how your feelings of self-worth and security will increase when you know you can take care of yourself.

When and When Not to Use Physical Defense

Knowing when to use physical-defense skills is just as important as knowing how. A knife in the hand of a surgeon can preserve life; a knife in the hand of a thug can end life. Self-defense skills used in life-threatening situations can save you. Self-defense skills used inappropriately can cripple both relationships and people. A clear head, a calm decision, and common sense are the simple items that you will add to your personal defense menu.

Some women who were immature, naive, and ignorant about the true purpose for learning self-defense enrolled in our clinics for wrong reasons. Here are a few actual quotes from such people:

> "I want to learn how to kick a man in the groin. My husband hits me and I want to teach him a lesson."

> "I want to learn a karate chop to smash my brother's nose if he sticks it in my business again."

> "I just hate men to harass me when I'm walking alone. Once I learn to fight, I won't have to tolerate their whistles and grabs."

If you have similar reasons for learning defense skills, please accept our word that you must adopt a more mature attitude before reading our book. We would not feel comfortable giving loaded guns to children. We do not want the responsibility of teaching skills to immature people who will not know how to use them properly. Thus you must share responsibility and develop the wisdom to know that these skills and techniques are to be used only against true assailants and in life-threatening situations.

Your Legal Responsibility

What is your legal responsibility for taking self-defense action? The California law states:

> It is lawful for a person who is being assaulted to defend himself from attack if, as a reasonable person, he has grounds for believing and does believe that bodily injury is about to be inflicted upon him. In doing so, he may use all force and means which he believes to be reasonably necessary and which would appear to a reasonable person, in the same or similar circumstances, to be necessary to prevent the injury which appears to be imminent.

While written in various forms, most state laws throughout the United States concur with the California law. The important phrases are: (1) The victim must believe that bodily injury is about to be inflicted. This judgment, according to Steward R. Rappaport, Chief of the Central Superior Court Trials Division in the office of the Public Defender in Los Angeles, can be made if the assailant is carrying a weapon, threatens you physically or verbally, or looks at you in a menacing way. (2) The victim may use all force and means that he believes to be reasonably necessary to prevent injury.

In addition, Los Angeles Superior Court Judge Earl Riley states, "A victim's attack must be commensurate with the assailant's intentions."

To illustrate the law: You are assaulted by a man near a police station. If you can immobolize him quickly and run to safety, it would be wrong to continue to kick him into unconsciousness. On the other hand, you are in the desert with a man who intends to kill you. Your car has broken down, and you must walk five miles to safety. Under these circumstances it is legal to continue to attack until you are certain the assailant is unconscious and will not recover until you reach safety.

Since many women are concerned about being sued by their assailants after incapacitating them, we asked Chief Rappaport if this was a possibility. When he stopped laughing he replied, "Can you imagine a 210-pound burly rapist suing a 105-pound frail female for defending herself while being assaulted?" He continued, saying that when you know you are in danger, fight! If you delay because you're worried about what might happen in court, it may be too late.

Strategy Versus Tactics

In learning self-defense, you need to adopt certain overall attitudes, goals, and plans. These we refer to as "strategies." Mental preparedness is essential. The specific things to do in a given dangerous situation—running, screaming, or kicking—are "tactics." What would be a good tactic to use in one situation may be totally useless or even dangerous in another. Thus, as you learn specific tactics of self-defense, keep in mind the need to be flexible and to apply them only as your general strategy indicates.

Here is an example—from a life-threatening situation—that may be helpful in showing the important difference between strategies and tactics in self-defense. Imagine that it is late at night and you are returning to your car in an isolated underground parking lot. Your arms are filled with packages. As you approach your car, a man suddenly leaps in front of you and grabs you in a tight bear hug. His eyes are glazed, and he is uttering obscenities. Your strategy is obvious: You must fight to gain your freedom from this madman and flee to safety. Your tactics are the following: Scream as loudly as you can, drop your packages, and deliver a forceful groin pull. In agony, he releases his hold, and you execute a double-hand blow to the back of his neck. He falls to the ground, and you immobilize him with kicks and run to safety.

With the proper strategy of mental and physical preparedness for self-defense, you could perform all of these simple tactics and escape quickly. Without proper mental and physical preparedness, you would have no strategy in this horrible situation and no tactical maneuvers to carry out. All you could do is pray that your assailant had enough mercy in his murderous soul to spare your life. If you had mastered the strategies and tactics presented in this manual, however, faith in yourself would be all that you would need. Your strategies would be clear and your tactics to achieve them obvious.

Chapter 2
Strategies for Self-defense

In this chapter we introduce the strategies of self-defense that you will learn in order to live safely. Many women believe that self-defense requires great physical skills and athletic prowess. On the contrary, only one of the three strategies of self-defense involves physical ability. This strategy is easily learned, requires almost no athletic ability, and can be mastered by old or young, agile or awkward, weak or strong. The three strategies of self-defense are:

1. Eliminate potential dangers.
2. Recognize and avoid dangers.
3. Fight—but only when necessary.

We suggested to our readers an acronym to help them remember these strategies. It has to do with the equal rights movement—namely, "E.R.A. Feminist." (Eliminate, Recognize and Avoid, and Fight.)

Because modern women live such varied lives, it is impossible for us to describe strategies and techniques applicable to each reader's unique life-style. For this reason, we have provided space on page 22 for you to list the five most dangerous situations that could occur in your life. Take into account your age, the neighborhood where you live, work, or attend school, how you travel, the people you regularly meet, and any special characteristics about yourself that could invite danger. Make the list more meaningful by writing in the first-person present tense. For example, "I am awakened from a deep sleep by a man crawling through my bedroom window." Or, "My car runs out of gas in a dangerous neighborhood and a gang of young thugs is surrounding it."

As you read the rest of this book, refer to these personal situations. We hope that our examples will help you to think of other dangerous situations that could happen to you. Let yourself freely imagine that you are in these situations and then overcome any anxiety they may cause you to feel. Later on as you read you will figure out ways to protect yourself. Action is the cure—not hiding your head in the sands of ignorance.

Eliminate Potential Dangers

By potential dangers we mean those situations that have not occurred and with proper planning will most likely never occur. The way to eliminate potential dangers is to develop proper psychological habits. *Think safety*. Bad psychological habits can give you a false sense of security.

Are we suggesting that you become a suspicious person? Yes! In Chapter 1 we explained some of the reasons why women have bad mental habits. These bad mental habits are denial, rationalization, and Victorian thinking. We use these bad mental habits to outwit ourselves. They must be consciously, purposefully, and continuously avoided. We don't want you to be the kind of victim who says, "If only I'd thought of that before, this would never have happened."

Let's take a look at a few of these bad habits in action. While reading up to this point in the book, did you think, "I don't have to read any more because none of this could ever happen to me." This thought is the product of the bad mental habit called denial. It comes from a desire to deny the painful feeling of anxiety that accompanies imagining yourself being attacked. To avoid denial you must acknowledge the anxiety that accompanies the thought "It can happen to me." Indeed it can and will more likely happen to you if you fail to face this fact and respond accordingly.

Return for a moment to the list you wrote of your five dangerous situations. Imagine how you might have eliminated these occurrences. In the first example we cited, proper window locks should have been installed. For summertime use, a device is available that allows windows to be opened only a few inches, thereby allowing air in for ventilation but keeping people out. In our second example, the danger could have been eliminated by keeping the car in top running condition. This means never allowing the gas tank to get less than one-quarter full, keeping up with regular maintenance, and repairing any problems immediately.

Many dangers can be eliminated by conveying to potential assailants that you have a self-assured attitude. Walk with assertiveness, direction, and purpose and convey the impression that you know where you are going. These actions can create reluctance in the mind of a potential assailant to approach you, thus eliminating potential danger before it can become an actual one. The assertive attitude that we are recommending can be portrayed when walking, standing, or even sitting. The way you keep your body held erect, the way your eyes watch intently rather than dart furtively or gaze inattentively, the confident way you hold your purse or packages are types of body-language messages that are easily read by potential assailants.

A recent television interview with a rapist focused on this subject of body language. The interviewer asked the assailant how he selected his victims. Without so much as a pause he said, "I like the type that I can dominate easily, so I pick out one that's walking slowly, without a sense of real direction, a type that looks like she'd be a pushover, you know what I mean?" Indeed, we do know what he means. Imagine how you look to others as you walk down the street. Then try to project the image of a self-assured, confident personality. You'll be surprised how easily and quickly others will recognize this body language emanating from you.

It is amazing how many dangerous situations you will be able to completely eliminate by thinking ahead. Worrying once and doing something to eliminate the danger prevents worrying over and over again. This then is the first strategy—eliminate potential dangers.

Recognize and Avoid Dangers

Even with the best mental preparedness and elimination of every potential danger you can imagine, threats to your personal safety can still occur. It goes without saying that the earlier you recognize danger, the earlier you can take corrective action. In fact, being alert can often prevent a dangerous situation from erupting and leading to a tragedy. Again, we must caution you that having the proper mental habits is the key to this strategy. It is amazing how many times we hear of women who were robbed or assaulted and did not allow themselves to realize their obvious exposure to danger—even after the danger began to develop. In fact, it is sometimes easier when real danger develops to deny its existence until it is too late. This occurs when the first feelings of panic, which should serve to alert you, lead to more denial. It may sound strange, but feelings of anxiety can be very helpful if you use them to signal impending danger.

Here is an example of how early recognition and avoidance work. Two young women, strangers to each other, are walking down a city street. One is thinking about a job interview to which she is hurrying. Her thoughts are: "Will the boss like me? What will he ask me? Am I dressed properly?" Thus preoccupied, she is oblivious to the following facts. The neighborhood she entered as she crossed the main boulevard has deteriorated. There are small alleyways leading off the street, the sidewalk is narrow, she is walking very close to the buildings, and there is no car traffic. But, most important of all, she does not "notice" that two tough-looking men have fallen in step behind her. Now let's look inside the mind of the second woman. As she hurried along, she "noticed" the neighborhood had deteriorated. She sensed potential danger from the small alleys and narrow sidewalks and thus walked along the curb. As soon as she saw the two men, her pulse quickened and she thought, "I may be in danger and I must do something to avoid it." Thus alerted, she looked for a place of safety. There, across the street, was a store. She immediately crossed the street and entered the store to wait until the men disappeared. As she waited, a shriek of terror came from the street. Looking through the store window, she witnessed the other woman being thrown to the sidewalk by one of the men, while the other grabbed her handbag. She then heard the echo of their footsteps down an alley as they ran away.

The woman who recognized and avoided danger was the one to help the victim to her feet and to give her a dime to call the police. She bore the fruits of the effort she had spent learning the strategy of self-defense. The other woman, unknowledgeable and unprepared to react properly, bore the pain and loss.

Another example illustrates how the strategy of recognizing and avoiding danger helped one of our readers. This woman, a college student, reported the following events. She shares a two-bedroom apartment next to the campus with a girl friend. Her neighborhood is considered safe; the building is new and has well-lighted halls and a locked entry from the street. In keeping with the first principle of self-defense, she had checked her apartment carefully and felt secure in knowing that she had eliminated all the potential dangers she could think of. One evening as her roommate was dressing to go out on a date, she decided to go shopping. Returning an hour later, she became anxious when she noticed her apartment door was ajar. Her first thought was that her roommate had forgotten to close it when she went out. This had never occurred before, because her roommate was also conscious of safety. All these observations added up to one conclusion—there may be a burglar inside.

Quietly she hurried to a neighbor's apartment and called the police. The dispatcher was courteous and understanding, and within a few minutes a police car pulled up to the apartment building. Accompanied by two police officers, she returned to her apartment where the door was still ajar. The officers asked her to wait in the hall. As they entered her apartment, she heard a commotion. Several minutes later three men emerged. One was handcuffed. She had just witnessed her first arrest. When the burglar came to trial, it was revealed that her roommate's date had failed to double lock the apartment door. This allowed the burglar to insert a plastic card between the door and the jamb and easily gain entrance into her apartment.

Another method of recognizing and avoiding danger is by not engaging in conversations with strangers. Rapists whom we have interviewed confided that they used the following ploys to attract the attention of potential victims: Asking for the time, getting into a prolonged discussion about directions, dropping an object in front of an intended victim and grabbing her when she begins to retrieve it, or pretending to have automobile trouble and flagging down the victim for assistance. One woman we interviewed was attacked as she was getting into her car in an underground parking garage. A man asked her if he could use his jumper cables on her car to get his car started. Not being mentally prepared, the woman said "yes." She told us later that she didn't want to be rude. If you sense potential danger, your last concern should be rudeness. This woman should have replied, "I'm in a huge rush but I will stop at the garage down the street and ask them to send help." It is possible to be polite and still recognize and avoid danger. For example, if a man asks you the time as you're walking down the street, simply look at your watch, tell him the time, and keep walking without further adieu. Or if someone asks for directions, give them quickly or say "I'm sorry, I don't know," and keep walking. Do not engage in conversation.

The task of recognizing and avoiding danger is never complete. You must always be alert to the possibility that new dangers can arise. Remember, if it's you, it's 100 percent. Such thoughts as "If only I had seen what was happening, I could have gotten away" are little consolation for stolen valuables, and they don't pay hospital bills if you are injured.

I, Mary Conroy, am frequently asked if I've ever had to fight with an assailant. No, I have not, but while studying for my doctorate at Columbia University in New York City I was robbed at knife point. Since then I have become a champion at recognizing and avoiding danger. For example, I recently had an appointment with a new dentist whom I had never met. His office was located on the top floor of the building. Entering the crowded elevator I pressed the button for the twelfth floor, noting that it had not already been pushed. At the eleventh floor everyone left the elevator except a strange-looking man who nervously stood in the corner. Reacting to my instinct, I stepped out just as the elevator doors closed and walked up the open staircase. I entered the office and was introduced to my doctor . . . who was none other than the strange-looking, nervous man in the elevator. We were both embarrassed, but that's OK. It is far better to suffer a little embarrassment than to suffer the results of a physical attack.

When danger is imminent and you are face to face with an assailant, there are still many ways to avoid physical contact. In the following section we describe tactics you can use in order to avoid fighting.

Tactics to Avoid Fighting

Run and scream. Upon recognizing danger, determine if you can outrun your assailant to a safe place. Since most women cannot outrun a man, try to seek safety close at hand. If you can run, scream "fire, fire" loudly to draw attention to your plight. Even if no one can hear, it will unnerve your assailant and possibly discourage his pursuit. Look back frequently enough to know whether he is gaining on you. If you cannot outdistance him, you will have to stop, turn, and attack (Figure 2–1).

FIG. 2-1a

2-1b

RUN, SCREAM, AND PREPARE TO FIGHT

FIG. 2-1c

2-1d,

2-1e,

2-1g

*(CONT'D) RUN, SCREAM,
AND PREPARE TO FIGHT*

Always run to where there are people. If you can reach a crowded street, mingle until you are certain that you are no longer pursued. Do not expect help from strangers. Newspaper stories of women being attacked in plain view of passersby and no one coming to their aid are unfortunately too common. If people aren't around, run to an open area. Avoid isolated places. If you are fleeing at night, the same rules apply, but in addition you should run toward lighted areas. Exposure is your ally.

Talk. Imagine yourself face to face with a criminal and you can't run. The chips are down, your heart pounds, and you are terrified. Your best defense at this point is talking. Say "What do you want?" You may determine that your assailant is a robber. If so, offer no resistance and give him your valuables. Most robbers don't want to harm victims; they just want to rob them and get away. If you determine that he is a rapist, you may be able to dissuade him. We know of a woman who talked her way out of being raped by saying she had cancer of the vagina. By talking to an assailant, you can also gain time to calm yourself, assess your predicament, and plan your attack. In addition, talking will help preserve your best weapon of attack—surprise.

Fight When Necessary

The third strategy of self-defense is physical attack. Knowing when to attack is as important as knowing how to attack. As we have indicated, there are many ways to avoid actual attack when you are faced with an assailant. Only when these fail is physical attack necessary or warranted. Of the three self-defense strategies, attack is the only one that requires physical skill and training. The techniques for attack that we recommend are simple to master, require little strength, and allow you to escape. They are tailored to individual situations and range from defending against a forceful intruder to totally incapacitating a would-be murderer. *The tactic you select must match the danger to which you are exposed!* The following events will take place once you determine an attack is necessary.

Planning Your Attack

Planning your attack includes choosing your best weapons and the most vulnerable areas of your assailant's body. This is not as complicated as it may sound because you have only five weapons that we recommend (Figure 2–2), and there are only four vulnerable areas that we suggest you attack.

Your Five Weapons

Voice. Every time you physically counterattack, scream. We shall stress this in discussing all tactics of self-defense. It is important to remember that a piercing scream can distract and unnerve an assailant. It may also alert others to your plight. We are not referring to yelling "help." We are referring to an aggressive, terrifying, loud, long yell.

Fingers and thumbs. Your fingers and thumbs are your best weapons when used properly because they can severely injure an assailant. In Chapter 4 we discuss gouging the eyes with the thumbs and jabbing the eyes with the fingers—two self-defense techniques that are incapacitating and life-saving. The common TV and movie stereotype of a woman scratching at an assailant is good for selling movies and promoting TV shows, but it is not the way to use these weapons.

Hands. Your hands are used when executing two techniques; first, the groin pull, and second, the double-hand blow to the neck. Correct positioning of the hands is necessary for the double-hand blow. The movie or TV picture of the woman who makes a fist and strikes down a man is based on pure fantasy. In reality though it can be done with proper hand positions.

Knees. Delivering a knee blow to the groin is a very effective way to immobilize an assailant. Learning the proper use of your knee adds an important weapon to your arsenal of self-defense.

Legs. Your legs are the strongest part of your body. They are longer and offer more leverage, their muscle mass is greater, and they can deliver more forceful blows. Also, you are more likely to catch an assailant by surprise with a kicking attack, which has less chance of being blocked. Kicking, however, is the most difficult skill we recommend and will require practice to make perfect.

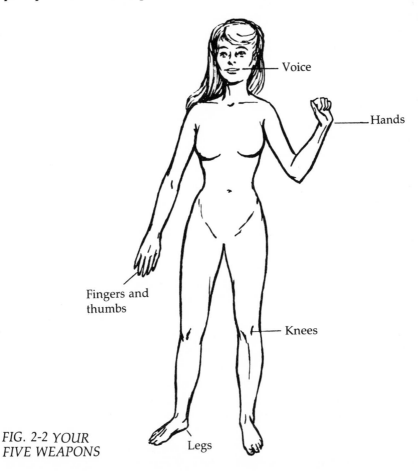

FIG. 2-2 YOUR
FIVE WEAPONS

Your Four Targets

As we mentioned before, there are four areas of a man's body that we will teach you to attack (Figure 2–3). Our research shows that an appropriate attack to one of these four most vulnerable areas will result in serious injury to an assailant.

Of course, there are many other targets on the body that if hit properly could hurt an assailant. We are often asked why we do not recommend these targets. The answer is simple: Never just hurt—always injure your assailant. If your attack does not immobilize the assailant, you will only aggravate him and he will counterattack more viciously than before. To illustrate this point, many self-defense "experts" recommend stamping on a man's instep or kicking him in the shin. Even if the shin or instep is hit directly, most women can only cause pain and little injury, which will simply aggravate the assailant. A man who physically assaults a woman is, at that moment, an aggressive, hostile, hateful person who has but one concern—himself. If you "hit him just a little" to let him know that you "mean business," he may kill you. We have interviewed numerous assailants and posed this question: "What would you do if a woman whom you are attacking kicked you in the shin or stomped on your instep?" Each concurred that he would knock her "blankety-blank" head off or smash her to the ground.

We cannot stress enough that you will only be fighting an assailant in a life-threatening circumstance and that you must be fully prepared to seriously injure and incapacitate him so that you can make your escape. The more simple and direct your attack, the more effective it will be. In keeping with this philosophy, we recommend only the following four target areas.

Eyes. The most vulnerable areas of your assailant's body, whether a man, woman, child, or vicious animal, are the eyes. If you are fighting to save your life, you should have no compunction about directing your attack to the eyes. When we make this statement to women, they usually wince and complain that it sounds very vicious. It is indeed vicious, but you have to be vicious in order to save your life. An attack to the eyes results in immediate, severe, immobilizing pain and possible damage of either a temporary or permanent nature. The fact that this damage may be permanent is of no concern to you when it comes to saving your life. Blinding an assailant has the added advantage of protecting you during your escape.

Groin. The second most vulnerable area for attack is the groin. The male genital organs (commonly referred to as the testicles, balls, or scrotum) are external and readily accessible to attack. The pain that a man receives from being struck in the groin takes his breath away, makes it impossible for him to stand upright, and can totally immobilize him. A groin pull, as opposed to an attack to the eyes, is less likely to result in permanent damage.

FIG. 2-3 YOUR FOUR TARGETS

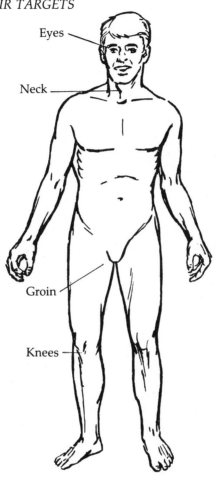

Knees. The knee is a very complicated and delicate anatomical structure. Although the knee can sustain great force during running or sports activities, it is a hinge that is designed to bend in only one direction. Even slight force applied against the front or side can sever tendons, rupture the discs, and cause dislocation of bones. To illustrate, your knee can bend from a straight to an almost 180-degree position toward the rear but cannot bend forward from a straight position. The patella, or kneecap, offers little protection from blows coming from the front and no protection from blows coming from the sides. Approximately forty pounds of pressure will snap a knee joint. Forty pounds is really a small amount of pressure for you to exert, considering that your legs support your body. Students ask if they can cause damage to an assailant if they are barefooted. It makes no difference.

Neck. Striking an assailant's neck can lead to temporary immobilization or unconsciousness. A blow on the back of the neck can injure the spinal column, causing an assailant to black out. This blow is used as a secondary target. For example, if a properly delivered knee to the groin results in the assailant's doubling over and exposing the back of his neck, you will be able to easily deliver a double-hand blow to this secondary target.

Delivering Your Attack

Speed, accuracy, force, and follow-through are necessary ingredients for a successful attack. Let us examine each of these factors independently.

Speed. Once you are sure that your life is in danger and that you must fight, the speed with which you carry out your attack is crucial. Rapid movements protect your main advantage, the element of surprise. The speed with which you deliver blows increases their momentum and overall effectiveness. Also the quicker you are, the less chance your assailant has to block or dodge your attack.

Accuracy. Hitting your target is crucial. Practice is necessary if you are to learn to deliver gouges, blows, kicks, and jabs on target. This takes time, patience, and practice. Remember, a kick a few inches above or below the knee can cause pain but will not immobilize an assailant. In Chapter 10 we recommend several techniques to help you perfect your accuracy.

Force. The laws of physics teach that the velocity of an object is more important than its weight in determining the force it can deliver. Translated into simple terms, a rapidly moving jab from the small hand of a woman can deliver much more force than the slow-moving punch from a large-fisted man.

Follow-through. Every successful attack must include follow-through. This means that your attack has to continue until your assailant is immobilized and you can escape to freedom. Follow-through should be conducted during each practice period until it becomes second nature.

To illustrate the importance of "following through until the assailant is totally incapacitated," consider the following true story. While conducting research for the Los Angeles Police Department, I (Mary Conroy) was assigned to interview police women throughout the country regarding self-defense techniques. A New York City police woman told of how she was accosted in her apartment by a man who crawled through her bathroom window. She was a martial artist and delivered a single-hand blow to his throat. The man reeled back across her bed as she raced to her front door, which was secured with four locks. She had unlocked three as the assailant recovered and flew at her in a rage. Having lost her element of surprise, she was severely beaten and left for dead. Her recommendation: "Never just strike an assailant once. While he's stunned with your first blow, hit him with your second and continue your attack until you're certain he can't retaliate. I learned that the hard way."

Summary

In this chapter we have described your three strategies for self-defense. We wish to stress that you must (1) eliminate potential danger by thinking ahead and taking appropriate actions, (2) be aware of yourself in relationship to your immediate surroundings so that you can quickly recognize and avoid dangers, and (3) learn when and how to physically defend yourself. We introduced you to only five of your bodily weapons and suggested that they be aimed at only four targets on an assailant's body. Simplicity and directness are the key factors in the Conroy Method of Self-defense. (Specific tactics are described in Chapter 4.)

My Five Dangerous Situations

1. _____
   _____
   _____
   _____
   _____
   _____

2. _____
   _____
   _____
   _____
   _____
   _____

3. _____
   _____
   _____
   _____
   _____

4. _____
   _____
   _____
   _____
   _____

5. _____
   _____
   _____
   _____
   _____

Chapter 3
The Golden Rules of Personal Safety

To live as safely and securely as possible requires forethought and planning. In this chapter we present a series of suggestions that together make up the golden rules of personal safety. While some of these suggestions may seem overly cautious, remember the old adage: "An ounce of prevention is worth a pound of cure." Part of the research for this chapter included interviewing burglars and robbers. Many of our suggestions are based on what they told us.

Free, expert advice regarding home safety is sometimes available by simply calling your local police station. Crime-prevention officers who are knowledgeable about local crime conditions can provide valuable assistance. In fact, that's their job—to educate and assist citizens. We always encourage our students to call the police and become acquainted with them "before they are needed."

Precautions in the Home

Install Safety Devices

Proper door and window locks. When moving into a new home or apartment, have a reliable locksmith change all the outside door locks.

This is necessary because a former tenant can enter by using old keys.

Most home and apartment doors have spring or snap locks. This type can easily be jimmied with a plastic card or ruler. If you have this type of ineffective lock, replace it at once with a dead-bolt lock for maximum security. (See Figure 3–1.) To emphasize the importance of this point, let us tell you of a police officer who attended one of our classes. He made the statement that he could open a door with a credit card faster than any student could with a key. All the students doubted this and were amazed to find that, in fact, he could when put to the test.

SPRING LATCH

Many homes and apartments have entrance locks with spring latches. This type is relatively simple for the burglar to open. He merely slides in a piece of celluloid or a knife blade and pushes back the latch. This type of latch is recommended for interior doors only.

DEADLOCKING LATCH

For a few extra cents, **Weiser** locks can be equipped with a deadlocking latch. This latch has a small bar alongside the latch bolt. When the door is closed, the bar pushes into the locking mechanism and prevents the latch bolt from being forced back.

DEAD BOLT

Maximum security is achieved by the addition of a dead bolt with 1" throw slightly above the regular lock on the door. This is a heavy unbevelled bolt with a free-turning steel bar in the center. The would-be intruder cannot manipulate such a bolt or cut it with a hack saw.

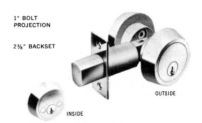

1" BOLT PROJECTION

2⅜" BACKSET

OUTSIDE

INSIDE

DOUBLE CYLINDER DEADLOCK

Locked or unlocked by key from either side. Dead bolt automatically deadlocks when fully extended. The attaching bolts are from inside only.

FIG. 3-1 (CONT'D)
TYPES OF LOCKS.

CYLINDER DEADLOCK WITH BLANK PLATE

Locked or unlocked by key from outside only. Blank plate inside. Dead bolt automatically deadlocks when fully extended.

CYLINDER DEADLOCK WITH THUMB TURN

Locked or unlocked by key from outside and by thumb turn on inside. Dead bolt automatically deadlocks when fully extended.

Chain locks should be used on the inside of your doors for added protection. Be sure that the chain is short enough to prevent an intruder from slipping his hand in and removing it. Keep in mind that a chain lock can be forced open by a determined intruder. The sound of the chain breaking, however, will alert you to the danger at hand. Also remember that a lock is only as strong as the door that it secures. Outside doors should be solid core or metal, and two- or two and one-half-inch screws should be used to secure door and window frames.

Windows are frequent entryways for burglars. There are many window locks and devices on the market that limit how far a window can be opened. One should be installed on every window that a burglar could reach. There are also inexpensive alarms that allow you the best of both worlds—safety and ventilation. These noise alarms can be set to trigger when a window is opened beyond a certain point. Most hardware stores carry them or can give you information about where they can be purchased. The models we have seen are all self-installed and require no alterations to your house or apartment.

Sliding glass doors and windows can be secured by placing a broom handle on the bottom in the groove. However, with effort, a broom handle can be dislodged. Therefore, for maximum protection, install a slide bolt that locks with a key.

If you have outside doors with outward-facing hinge posts, you can secure them by "pinning." To pin a hinge, you must remove two opposite screws and drive a finishing nail into the door side, protruding one-half inch. Drill a one-inch hole on the opposite or house side of the hinge. Thus, when the door is closed, the nail will cross from the door into the wall and prevent a burglar from pulling the door out after removing the hinge post.

If you live on the ground floor of a house in a high-risk neighborhood, you may want to use bars on the windows. They should be installed on the inside of the house where a burglar cannot reach them and they must have escape latches in case of fire.

Electronic warning system. Over the past decade many electronic warning systems have been developed for the home. If you live in a high-crime neighborhood, if your home is isolated from view, or if you have many valuables to protect, such a system may be worth the expense. You can find the names of companies that install these warning systems in the Yellow Pages of your phone directory under the heading "Burglar alarm systems."

Through-the-door viewer. Many robbers and assailants gain entry to homes by simply lying. They will claim to be repairmen, gas men, or neighbors. To avoid such deceptions, you should install a through-the-door viewing device so that you can see who is at your door. These viewers are inexpensive and easily installed. Always use the viewer before opening the door. Don't be fooled by a uniform or business suit. If you don't recognize a caller, there are a few things you should do. If he says he represents a utility company or repair service, have him show you his company identification card. If you are suspicious, phone the company for verification. An honest employee will not feel offended. Do not phone the number he offers; look up the company's number in your phone book. If he does not work for the company or has not been dispatched to your home, phone the police at once.

As an added precaution, it is wise to make appointments for repairs or installations when you have company, preferably a man.

It may help you to be aware of some common ruses that criminals have used to gain entry into homes. They are:

> "I'm an undercover police officer investigating a robbery in this building, and I'd like to ask you a few questions."
> "I'm doing road construction down the street. May I have a glass of water."
> "My car just broke down in front of your house. May I use your phone."
> "I'm delivering flowers to you, and you have to sign for them."

When strangers appear to deliver packages that you are not expecting, be suspicious. Though it may seem awkward, we recommend that you request that the package be left on the doorstep. Wait until you are certain the delivery man has departed before fetching your package. If you are asked to sign a receipt, have it passed under the door or through the mailbox. If this is impossible, verify on the phone with his company that he is indeed dispatched to your home. Once again, get the company's number from your phone book; don't take his word for it because he may give you the number of an accomplice. Simply telephone.

We know of a woman living alone who had the habit of calling loudly "I'll get the door, Rocky" whenever she answered her doorbell. This created in the mind of her caller the illusion that she was not alone.

Many students point out that they would make an exception to this rule of not letting strangers into their house if someone claimed there was an emergency and wished to call the police. We caution you against this possible trick. It is a simple matter to get the information from a person at your door and call the proper authorities yourself. A dramatic example occurred in California. Police reports indicate that Patricia Hearst's abductors first knocked on her door and asked to use the telephone because of an emergency. Once inside the house, they proceeded to kidnap her.

Some women foolishly leave their door unlocked when expecting a deliveryman. This is not only an invitation to a burglar but may even encourage thefts or sexual advances from trusted workers.

Don't give your keys to service people such as painters, repair men, or installers. Even though the businessman you know may be trustworthy, he could have employees who will duplicate your keys to use or sell them.

Avoid giving your key to the building superintendent. If your lease requires that you do so, take the following precautions: Place the key in an envelope and seal it in such a way that you can tell if it has been opened. Signing your name across the seal, using clear plastic tape, or using candle dripping on the flap will help to ensure safety. Be certain to inform the superintendent that he must let you know if he uses the key. Your landlord should be glad to cooperate because if your apartment is burglarized he can easily prove his non-involvement by producing the sealed envelope.

Don't aid burglars by leaving ladders against your house or tools exposed. Several convicted felons whom we interviewed chuckled as they told us how irresistible such "made to order" situations were for them.

Protecting the perimeter of your house is just as important as locking your front doors. Garden gates, passageways between houses, carports, and crawl spaces under buildings should be carefully studied to see if they leave you vulnerable. Garage doors can be secured by automatic door-opening devices, double locking, or hardened-steel padlocks. Be sure to remove any identifying numbers on the locks to prevent a burglar from ordering his own keys.

New inventions in electronics and mass marketing have made heat and smoke detectors readily available. Since several excellent types may suit your needs, we recommend that you call your local fire department and ask their advice. In many cities a fire-prevention officer will come to your home without charge to identify the most efficient places to install your units.

Properly Dispose of Keys and Valuables

Keys. Frequently women unwittingly undo their efforts to have their home securely locked. For example, to avoid locking themselves out they hide a key in a "secret" place. This presents a problem in that there are few secret places to hide a key. A doormat, mailbox, windowsill, or milk box are obvious to both you and a burglar. If you are worried about being locked out and need a safety valve, it is best to leave a key with a trusted friend or neighbor.

Another word of caution about your house keys. Don't keep them on the same ring as your car keys. Many successful burglars operate by having parking-lot attendants duplicate house keys while a car is parked. Some women make it easier for burglars by putting name and address tags on their key rings. If you place an identification tag on your key, use an office address or street number other than your home address. If your purse containing keys and identification is lost or stolen, have the house lock changed immediately.

Cash. Most people realize that it is unwise to keep large sums of cash at home. If you have valuables, avoid hiding them in cookie jars, dresser drawers, or under mattresses. These are places where burglars usually look first. If, however, circumstances necessitate that you keep a large sum of cash at home overnight, we offer the following suggestion. Place the cash in an envelope, insert the envelope under the label of a package of frozen food or inside an ice cream container, and put this package in the back of the freezer compartment of your refrigerator. In case of burglary or a fire, your money will be safe, unless of course the burglar has read this book or has a super-case of the munchies.

Important papers. Stock certificates, birth certificates, wills, copies of important papers, and credit card numbers should be kept in a bank safety-deposit box. It is also important to keep a record of the make and serial number of appliances, TV sets, automobiles, and other valuable items. On page 43, record this information, which will aid the police in identifying these items if they are stolen. Permanent marking, with your social security number or driver's license number, can easily be written on your appliances with electric metal markers, which can often be obtained at no cost from your local police department. This number makes merchandise easy to identify and therefore harder to fence. Furthermore, such numbered property makes irrefutable evidence in court. When you identify your property with an electric marking pencil, the police will also give you stickers to display on your doors and windows stating that you have joined "Operation Identification." This sticker will discourage burglars.

Along with marking your property, we suggest that you take

photographs of your valuables. Color closeups are preferable. They should be kept in a safety-deposit box or other fireproof location. Your insurance company may be willing to store these photographs for you.

Know Your Baby-sitter

When you leave your children with a sitter, make certain he or she is a responsible person. It is amazing how otherwise-concerned parents leave their most precious possessions, their children, in the care of total strangers. Never hire a baby-sitter from a newspaper advertisement or billboard in a shopping area. Always make personal inquiries about sitters. If it is not possible for you to find a baby-sitter or someone on whom you can get references, go to a reputable and bonded agency. When the sitter from an agency arrives, make certain he or she has proper identification. Instruct your sitter in safety measures as carefully as you would give instruction in child-care routines.

Discourage Break-ins

One way to discourage prowlers around your house or apartment is to keep outside lights turned on throughout the night in areas such as hallways, alleys, and secluded walkways. We are aware that this is a time when our country is concerned with saving energy, and there is much publicity to that effect. However, penny-wise is still pound-foolish, and the small expense of keeping a light on over a doorway can be a life-saving measure. A few years ago the Los Angeles Police Department mounted an information campaign with billboards pointing out the safety advantages of keeping a light on all night inside your home as well as over the entrance. Their campaign was based on information obtained from interviewing burglars and studying the pattern of their habits.

Maintaining the privacy of your home also needs some thought. Keep your drapes and shades drawn at night. If a potential assailant sees that you are alone, he is likely to attempt to enter.

When you are alone, there are several things you can do to create the illusion that you have company. For example, play a radio or TV set in another part of the house, keep lights on in different rooms, and if you hear a strange noise, don't hesitate to talk loudly to an imaginary man. We know this is a good advice because recently one of our former students met us at an alumni party. She thanked us for the course and told how the lecture on the rules of safety had been particularly helpful. One night while watching TV, she heard a noise outside her patio. Remembering our advice, she immediately thought up three imaginary friends and said, "Rocky, Vince, Sal, I heard a noise in the garden. Would you guys check it out for me?" Within seconds she heard footsteps running across the garden and down the alley behind her house.

When away from home, make it appear as though someone is there by leaving lights and the radio on. The price of the electricity will pay for your peace of mind.

Cooperate with a Burglar

What is the most sensible thing to do if you are confronted by a burglar in your home? We urge you to cooperate in every way you can. Make sure that he understands that you will give him anything he wants, and try to calm your own fears with the knowledge that most burglars just want to "take the money and run." A professional burglar is not interested in harming you. Be sure to observe his physical characteristics, anything he touched where fingerprints may be left, and how he made his escape. The details of how to make these observations and report them are discussed in Chapter 6 and Chapter 9.

During a robbery, attempt to keep your wits about you.

> "Is Marcy home?"
> "Huhn, wha'd you say?"
> "Tell her Jane dropped by to say hello, but I really can't wait."

With these words, a quick-witted student of ours fled from her own apartment and the strange man who had broken in. Most women upon finding someone in their apartment would think first of protecting their possessions rather than themselves. In this instance, our student, recognizing that she was in danger and placing her personal safety first, applied the second strategy of the Conroy Method—she avoided danger by thinking, talking, and fleeing.

Inform Police of Suspicious Entries

Women have reported that they suspected someone had entered their home or apartment when they were away. For example, a secretary told us that a jealous boyfriend would ransack her apartment occasionally. A professional dancer mentioned that a prior tenant had a key and would return to riffle through her record collection. An airline stewardess described a more difficult situation in which she suspected that her landlord periodically entered her apartment to rummage through her underclothing. She wanted to know how to confirm her suspicions. We suggested that she take a small piece of paper, fold it several times into a flat wedge, and insert it between the door jamb and the closed door from the outside approximately one inch above the floor. Upon returning home, she could then learn whether the door had been opened by noticing where the paper was. If it was lying on the floor, she would have evidence that someone had entered her apartment. To conclude this story, the inconspicuous piece of paper confirmed her suspicions and led to police apprehension of the landlord in her bedroom. She moved to a new apartment, he was ordered to have psychiatric treatment, and our story had a safe outcome.

Rely on the police, and overcome any reluctance to call them if you observe something suspicious. There are several reasons why people are reluctant to call the police. We are told by women, for example, that they don't want to seem "stupid." Or they are afraid of "getting involved because somebody may get back at me." Sometimes they are just afraid, for undefinable reasons, to have anything to do with the police. These types of reactions are self-defeating when looked at objectively. We must maintain our basic faith and trust in our police officers. This is done by extending our hands to them for help. Police would much rather prevent crimes than solve them.

Prepare for a Leave or Vacation

When you are away from home for a prolonged period of time, it may be worthwhile to find a house-sitter. A relative, trusted friend, or college student might enjoy the privacy and change of scenery afforded by such an offer. When you can find such a trusted person, instruct him or her in safety precautions so that you can relax and enjoy your vacation knowing that your home is properly cared for. If you must leave your home unattended, take the following steps to create the illusion that you are there.

Stop deliveries. A growing pile of newspapers by your front door is just a flashing neon sign saying "Empty house, enter at will." The mailman, milkman, dry-cleaning delivery man, and all routine delivery people should be notified to discontinue service. Do not tell them you are leaving town or exactly when to recommence service. This information could fall into the wrong hands.

Notify the police. The police are appreciative when told in advance that a home or an apartment will be vacant. They will check frequently and be extra alert for any clues that intruders are present. Be sure to tell them where you can be reached in an emergency.

Order vacation phone service. Many people are unaware of a phone service that reduces your rate and still allows the phone to ring in the usual manner when you are away. The phone company's business office will arrange for this service. Never disconnect your phone, because such false economy can serve as an advertisement that you are away.

Have yard work attended to. To successfully maintain the illusion that you are home, it is necessary to have the routine front yard and garden chores attended to. Make arrangements to have the grass cut, the hedges trimmed, the lawns sprinkled, and outside light bulbs replaced if they burn out.

Use an on-off lighting device. Disguising the fact that you are not at home takes more imagination than simply turning on the porch light. To test this fact for yourself, next time you're walking through your neighborhood at night try to determine which families are home and which just went out and left the porch light on. The illusion that you are at home at night can be created by purchasing an electric or clock-driven device that turns houselights off and on automatically. These devices are available at hardware or electrical-appliance stores and cost less than fifteen dollars. Use photosensitive switches to turn outside lights on at sunset and off at dawn. Keep blinds and drapes closed.

Let a neighbor know. A final precaution is to let a trusted neighbor know of your vacation plans. Tell him you have informed the police of your trip, and request that he notify them if he sees anything unusual in or about your property.

Form a neighborhood watch. You can assist yourself and your local police by joining a neighborhood watch program. These educational programs are sponsored by police departments throughout the country and have developed helpful material, including lectures, films, and demonstrations. Cooperation from neighbors results in increased safety by teaching people how to react to suspicious strangers and unusual sounds. If you are interested in establishing a watch in your neighborhood, the National Sheriffs' Association will send you a starter kit that includes a security checklist and decals for watch members to post on doors and windows as warnings to would-be burglars. Send $1.50 to the National Neighborhood Watch Program, National Sheriffs' Association, 1250 Connecticut Ave. N.W., Washington, D.C. 20036; or call (202) 872-0422.

Phone Precautions

Prepare for emergencies. The telephone can be your salvation in many emergencies. As with all safety factors, preplanning is the key to success. The following precautionary measures are important.

Tape two dimes (or the amount of a telephone call) in a convenient part of each of your purses for emergencies that can arise when only a pay phone is handy.

Keep a list of emergency numbers, such as the police, paramedics, ambulance service, fire department, and your private physician, both in your purse and by your phone.

For maximum-security purposes, you can request a separate telephone line with an unlisted number in addition to your regular phone. Although this is expensive, it offers certain advantages. For example, most burglars are clever enough to take a phone off the hook, thus rendering any extensions useless.

If an emergency arises and you are not able to dial directly for help, call the operator. He or she is trained to assist you. When making an emergency call, give the following information slowly and clearly: (1) your name, (2) the nature of the emergency, (3) the phone number and address from which you are calling, and (4) what type of assistance you think is necessary. Do not hang up until you have given all the necessary information.

Ward off obscene callers. Your telephone can also be a source of danger. Obscene phone calls are not only annoying but can lead to danger. They are most often made by sexual perverts or by adolescents who are seeking vicarious pleasures. Sexual perverts are sick people who often act out their sexual fantasies by talking about sex with unseen women. Sometimes their sickness dictates that they need to do more than just talk. In such cases they try to find out who you are and where you live. They are encouraged by the slightest response on your part. Thus, we urge you to hang up immediately. In the event that you have repeated obscene calls, try one of these tactics:

Tap on the mouthpiece with your fingernail or a pencil. This sounds as though the call is being traced. As you tap on the mouthpiece, say "Officer, this is the pervert who has been calling me, and now you can trace his line." Immediately hang up and notify the phone company.

Keep a police or gymnasium whistle near the phone. The minute you detect a pervert is on the line, blow the whistle directly into the mouthpiece. As soon as your line is free, notify the phone company and the police, because making obscene phone calls is a felony.

If these tactics fail, have your number changed to an unlisted number.

Protect your privacy. To prevent persistent telephone problems, here are some tactics to protect your privacy:

Have an unlisted phone number.

If you need to be listed, have the phone company use only the initials of your first and middle names so that you do not appear in the directory as a woman living alone. Also ask the phone company to remove your address from the telephone book. The less information printed about you, the safer you will be. So many women list their numbers using initials that obscene callers may assume that these numbers are women's. The advantage is that the obscene caller can't address the woman by her first name.

Never reveal to a caller that you are alone. For example, a stranger may ask a girl for her mother or father. She should say that her parents are unable to come to the phone, request the person's name and phone number, and say that they will return the call as soon as possible.

If you receive a wrong-number call, do not disclose your phone number. It is better to ask for the number the person called and then say "You have reached a wrong number," and hang up.

If it is necessary to place your phone number in an advertisement or on a public sign, avoid using your first name, address, or title such as "Miss," "Mrs." or "Ms." The less you advertise that you are a woman, the safer you will be.

Elevator Advice

To you an elevator is a convenience. For a would-be robber or rapist, it is a made-to-order cage in which to trap a victim. An elevator can be a trap because it is easily stopped between floors, is confining, and is practically soundproof. In view of these facts, the following precautionary measures are important whenever you enter an elevator.

Never get on an elevator with a suspicious-looking person. It is wiser to wait for the next car. If a suspicious-looking person enters after you, step out and wait.

Before entering an elevator, make sure that the direction light indicates it is going your way. It is safer to wait for a return car than to go to a roof or basement, because these are the places where assailants wait for victims. When riding with a stranger, try to stay next to the control panel. Then, if you suspect trouble, it is easier to push the alarm and also the button for the next floor so that you can get right off.

If a suspicious-looking person is lurking in the hallway, don't get off the elevator.

Car Cautions

When you are in your car, you should have an overall strategy for maintaining personal safety. Here is a list of precautions that are as important as good driving habits.

Keep your car in tip-top running condition. Never let your gas tank get less than one-quarter full. Have the oil, water, battery, fan belt, water hoses, and tires checked regularly when having your gas tank filled. These precautions take only a few minutes of the attendant's time but can save hours of delay and keep you out of danger.

Learn how to change a flat tire.

Avoid traveling on deserted roads. It is better to spend a few extra minutes of driving time in order to stay on a main highway.

When alone in a car, keep the doors locked and the window rolled up, and use the ventilation system to control the temperature. If you must keep a window open, use the one next to you so that it can be quickly raised if necessary. If you drive a convertible, keep the top up while driving alone.

Never hitchhike or offer rides to strangers. A young woman standing on a street corner with her thumb out is called "rape bait." When you hitchhike, you might as well have a sign around your neck saying "I am available for attack," and you must recognize that to some people you are implying availability. To illustrate this point, it is almost impossible for a woman to convince a jury that she has been raped if she voluntarily entered a man's car while hitchhiking. Many students have told us that they feel safe hitchhiking if they only accept rides from other women. They are foolhardy. We are quite blunt in pointing out to them that hitchhiking and accepting a ride from anyone is dangerous. Women can and do attack other women. Men can hide in a car. Men can disguise themselves as women and pick up women. Our advice also extends to the opposite situation: Never pick up a hitchhiker. Many people accept rides as hitchhikers and then rob or assault the well-meaning woman who picked them up. We are against hitchhiking in any form or manner.

If you are followed by someone in a car, drive deliberately, cautiously, and without excessive speed. Do not try to outmaneuver him, because chances are that you will wind up in a wreck. An assailant who chases his victim in a car may be a very skilled driver or intoxicated by liquor or drugs. In either case we advise you not to attempt to outmaneuver him. Instead, honk your horn to attract attention and drive to the nearest police station or into a well-lighted gas station.

If you pass a stranded motorist, even a woman, be a good samaritan by not stopping. Do yourself and the stranger a favor by driving to the nearest phone and calling the police. This may seem like cruel, heartless advice, but police files are filled with examples of how good samaritans have been lured into robbery and rape by supposedly "stranded" motorists.

Always lock your car doors, even when leaving for only a short time. If you find that your car locks have been tampered with or that your car has been broken into, it is important to report these facts to the police.

Avoid leaving valuables in your car. If you must do so, place them in the trunk or hide them from sight under the seat.

At night, if you cannot park close to your destination, try to find a parking lot or a well-lighted area. When you return to the car, make sure that you are not being followed. Always have your car keys ready. Check to see that no one is hiding in the back seat, enter quickly, and lock the door.

Don't stop for gas or directions in a neighborhood that looks dangerous.

Keeping the registration visible on the steering column is a dangerous practice and no longer required by law. Keep it locked in the glove compartment.

Some people put duplicate car keys in a magnetic box under the bumper or hood of their car. Neither we nor insurance companies recommend this practice. If you are worried about losing your keys, it is better to keep a duplicate set at home, at work, or with a trusted friend.

If you are stranded in your car on a well-traveled highway, freeway, or toll road, put on your four-way flashing emergency light, tie a white handkerchief to the aerial, lift the hood, get back into the car, lock the doors, and wait for help to arrive. If you are on a local road and in sight of a telephone or service station, put your flashing lights on, tie a white handerchief to the aerial, lock the car, and walk on the left-hand, curb side of the road or sidewalk. Walk facing traffic because it is safest. Experience has also proved that it is safer to remain with your car if you are stranded in a desolate area or in a storm. Be sure to open the windows slightly for ventilation, and run the engine intermittently only if you need to keep warm. If a stranger stops, do not accept a ride from him or her. In general, this can be as dangerous as hitchhiking. Instead, roll your window down a couple of inches, give the stranger change for a phone call, ask him or her to report your predicament to the police or a nearby garage attendant, and remain inside your car. A tragic example of a young girl who did not follow this advice occurred in Los Angeles. She was observed standing at her car by a highway patrolman who was cruising in the opposite direction on a freeway. Another passing motorist reported seeing her enter a car that had stopped, apparently to offer assistance. This young lady has never been seen or heard from since, and the incident occurred more than three years ago. Need we say more?

We recommend that every woman have a record of her license-plate number in her purse. Thus, in case your car is stolen, you can report your exact license numbers to the police. It is amazing how many people do not remember their own license-plate numbers.

Public Transportation

Airplanes

The threat of skyjacking has led to routine passenger and luggage searches. These precautions are necessary and well worth the inconvenience. To expedite boarding, check as much luggage as is possible. Carry on only items that can be easily opened for inspection. If you are skyjacked, remember that the crew is fully trained for such emergencies. Rely on their judgment and follow their instructions implicitly. Don't try to become a heroine.

Trains, Buses, and Subways

Stations for public transportation are tempting areas for assailants to find victims. Call ahead to find out time schedules and delays. By careful planning you can avoid long waits in these potentially dangerous areas. When waiting, stay in populated terminal areas such as the ticket booth or refreshment stand in view of uniformed employees. Never fall asleep in the station. After you have boarded, choose the aisle seat closest to the conductor or driver. From this seat you will be able to obtain help quickly if needed. Any unusual behavior by another passenger should be reported to the conductor or driver. If a suspicious-looking person is observing you and you know your station is in a deserted area, don't get off.

Taxis

When you are entering a taxi, note the driver's identification number and picture. Call him by name to ensure an "economic ride." Also make sure that he is following your directions. Several rape victims have reported that taxi drivers took them to desolate areas and that they didn't realize they were being diverted from their destination until just before being attacked. Another helpful suggestion is to request your driver to wait until you have safely entered your destination. We have never heard of a driver who wouldn't be glad to spend an extra minute or two when so requested.

Traveling Tips

More and more women today are traveling alone for business and pleasure. Here are some suggestions to make you feel more comfortable and safer when en route or in a distant city.

Planning Your Trip

Plan your trip as far in advance as you can. Use a travel agent or take advanced-reservation service provided by hotel chains to ensure that you have a place to stay. If you plan to arrive in the evening, be sure to obtain a "guaranteed reservation" by paying in advance or using a credit card.

Packing

When you are packing, remember that "least is best." It's amazing how many people lug appliances, unseasonable clothes, and other excess baggage so they won't be caught without something they consider vital. More often than not, they never use it. Take as little jewelry as possible and only those pieces that are inexpensive and to which you are not attached. There may be many keys to your hotel room, and you must assume that nothing left there is secure. If you must have valuables with you, check them in the hotel or motel safe.

Transportation

Transportation to and from home, plane, train, and bus depots can pose problems. If you are driving, park to minimize long walks through garages and open lots. Leave your car locked with no valuables in view in a well-lighted area. Avoid walking between narrow rows of parked cars where you are more vulnerable to attack. Walk briskly in well-lighted areas keeping your purse under your arm and luggage close to your body. Be aware of those about you. When returning to the parking lot, you may wish to identify yourself to the lot attendant. Tell him that if you haven't driven out within a reasonable length of time, he should call the police.

Identifying Luggage

The law requires that all luggage on airplanes be identified from the outside with the owner's name and address. We recommend that you do not use your home address because criminals have been known to use this ploy to learn addresses of people who are away. It is better to use your office or travel agent's address.

Meeting Strangers

There is a natural tendency to chat with strangers while traveling. In such conversations, don't indicate that you are traveling alone, don't disclose your hotel, and don't reveal the length of your trip. Should you want to meet your new acquaintance later, obtain his or her phone number and residence. If you are accused of being overly cautious, don't feel initmidated. When you reach the person later by phone, arrange to meet in public and do not place yourself in a vulnerable situation by meeting at a hotel room or residence.

If liquor is available, as on a plane, don't drink more than you can handle.

Your Hotel

Reserve a room in a reputable hotel or motel. The extra expense you may incur is worth your peace of mind. When you register, use your last name and initials of your first and middle. There are several ways to make your hotel room more secure. When leaving your room, turn on the television set, switch on the bathroom light, and place the bathroom door ajar. A "do not disturb" sign hanging from your locked hallway door may also discourage burglars.

Do not hesitate to ask the desk clerk or a police officer for advice about which parts of the city and means of transportation are safe.

When you return to your hotel room, look inside before entering. Before going to sleep, secure all locks and balance a chair against the door. If someone attempts to enter, the sound of the falling chair will awaken you. Keep in mind that numerous people have keys to your room. One New York hotel has only 1,500 rooms but loses 10,000 keys every year. Some are taken for souvenirs, some by mistake, and some by criminals.

Use the same precaution when answering the door of your hotel room as you would at home.

Leave Itinerary in Case of Emergency

Finally, leave your itinerary with a friend or relative in case of emergency. Also keep in touch by phone with someone at least every two days; thus if you are abducted your disappearance will be reported.

Public Area Precautions

Walk the Streets with Caution

Muggers and purse snatchers boldly attack women on sidewalks and in other public places. Here are several tactics to keep the odds in favor of your not becoming a victim.

Walk briskly with direction and confidence. If you feel threatened, imitate the walk of a professional football player. Appearing strong will lessen the possibility of your being attacked.

Walk on the curb side of the sidewalk, thus keeping maximum distance between yourself and alleyways in which assailants lurk.

Know exactly where you are going. Get complete directions and check a map before you leave for unfamiliar territory.

If you are being followed, cross the street at a 90-degree angle. Keep your pursuer in sight while you try to walk to safety. If he continues to follow you, scream "fire, fire" and run. If this doesn't dissuade him, drop your purse. If that's all he's after, you're safe.

If you must walk alone at night and cannot scream on cue, carry a noisemaker in your hand. The best noisemaker available is a compressed gas siren. Several types of sirens are available in department, hardware, and drugstores. If you don't have a siren, carry a whistle in your hand. Keep in mind, however, that it is difficult to blow a whistle while you are under stress.

Although a dog can be an expensive and time-consuming pet, it can provide protection. Even a small dog can deter a burglar or rapist by creating noise and alerting residents. A woman walking with a large dog is less vulnerable to assault on the street than one walking alone. Remember that strangers do not know how lovable or vicious your pet is. For example, we know a woman with a lovable, timid Samoyed that stands four feet tall. His name is Honeybun. Once she was out on the street and a drunk walked up to her and said something obscene. She yelled "Down Fang," and the drunk ran to the other side of the street.

Despite your desire to look fashionable, we advise you to cover up and look plain when out on the streets alone at night. A trip to the launderette, drugstore, or grocery store should not be used as an excuse to put on your scantiest outfit. If you are traveling alone to a date or a place where you must look presentable, wear an inconspicuous overcoat or wrap over your stylish clothes. A scarf around your head can also cover a new hairdo and make you look ordinary.

Sometimes the longest way around is the shortest way home, especially if there is an alley between you and the end of a block you must reach. A shortcut across the alley can put you in shadows and expose you to dangers from assailants. Stay in well-lighted areas. The same advice applies when you feel you are being followed. You may need to walk in the middle of a street or run screaming "fire, fire" to a populated area. Never run into an alley, hallway, or to your own residence.

When seeking help because someone is following you, persistence may be necessary. We know of a woman who was chased, ran to a lighted house, and pleaded to have the police called. The homeowner, not wanting to get involved, refused her help and demanded she get off his porch. Thinking quickly, she decided to get him involved, and picked up a potted plant and hurled it through his window. He phoned the police. The price of her safety was well worth the price she paid for his window.

Avoid Isolation

Avoid isolation in parks, restaurants, and theaters. Parks and recreational areas attract pleasure seekers as well as criminals and perverts. We suggest that you take the following precautions to discourage undesirable encounters in public places.

Avoid going to public areas alone, especially after dark, because a single woman is an easy target for trouble. When alone, patronize respectable, well-populated restaurants and theaters. Dress properly.

If you attend a movie or concert alone, sit next to a family or on an aisle. Avoid sitting in the last few rows of the orchestra or balcony.

Be certain that you are not being followed when you leave a theater or restaurant alone. If you are followed, return to the establishment for help.

Do not accept beverages or food from people you don't know.

If a stranger offers to escort you to your car or home, thank him and decline his offer.

If a stranger asks you a question, answer briefly as you walk away. If he persists, do not talk further. He may be giving you the vulnerability test with his questions—"Do you have change for a dollar?" "Got a light?" "I'm doing a survey . . ." Ignore him and walk briskly toward other people.

If while you are walking, a man in a car asks a question, do not approach the car. Answer briefly as you walk away. If he follows, simply reverse your direction.

Evade Exhibitionists

There is a specific form of sexual pathology in which a man gains both conscious and unconscious gratification from showing his genital organs to strangers. This type of pervert is commonly referred to as an exhibitionist or a "flasher." The illness occurs in men of all ages, races, and socioeconomic classes. These men are so beset with the impulse to expose themselves that they will do it in the most unlikely places and in the most irrational manner. When confronted by one, do not laugh at him or make demeaning comments—"sorry, sir, I haven't time to deal with your shortcomings." Rather say nothing and show no signs of outward emotion. We suggest that you simply look away, walk briskly to an area where there are other people, and report the incident to the police at once. There is a general stereotype that many of our students report concerning exhibitionists—namely, that they are harmless types of people who would not hurt them. Thus, they do not want to report them to the police. We know of no studies of exhibitionists that support such conclusions. They may or may not expose themselves before undertaking more serious assaults. Thus we advise you to report any such incidents to the police. Give as adequate a description of the exhibitionist as you can.

Watch Your Purse

An open purse invites danger. Most pickpockets and purse snatchers look for the opportunity to get near a woman carrying such a purse. When they find one, their job is easy. You can make their job difficult by carrying only purses with zippers or snap locks.

Purses have ways of walking away when placed on a store counter or in a shopping cart. Never leave yours alone. Always carry it close to your body. When sitting in a theater or on public transportation, your lap is the safest place for your purse. Also avoid displaying money in public places.

Summary

In this chapter we have given examples of how to assess potential dangers in your environment and daily routines. We also offered some suggestions on how to eliminate them. Give careful forethought to your own particular circumstances and life-style. Only you know what circumstances are potentially dangerous to you—only you can eliminate them.

RECORD OF VALUABLES

Automobiles, motorcycles, motor scooters, bicycles, etc.

Make	Serial No.	License No.	Color	Cost

Kitchen appliances: stove, dishwasher, blender, refrigerator, toaster, etc.

Make	Serial No.	License No.	Color	Cost

Radios, TVs, stereos, tape recorder, etc.

Make	Serial No.	License No.	Color	Cost

Watches, cameras, sports equipment, sewing machine, binoculars, etc.

Make	Serial No	License No.	Color	Cost

Chapter 4
Tactics for Defense

In Chapters 2 and 3 we emphasized strategies for eliminating and avoiding dangers. Now we ask you to imagine that these measures have failed and that you must fight to gain your freedom and save your life. There are no halfway attacks. You should not think, "I'll just hurt him a little bit," or "I'll just make him let go of me." Since your life is threatened, total, 100 percent attack is necessary. You should use all your knowledge, cunning, and physical skill to injure. Continue your attack until your assailant is incapacitated. Anything you do to save your life is morally and legally justified.

Mental Preparedness

To master specific techniques of attack, it is best to have a partner. We recommend that you get together with a friend or relative to practice. If this is difficult, then you must use your imagination. During practice picture yourself being attacked by a burly thug. Several victims of attacks have told us that they had not realized ahead of time how strong an assailant could be. Reassuringly, however, they were astounded by their own strength and ability to do what they had learned. They said that having imagined themselves attacked during training was the single most valuable thing that helped them, which proves that one cannot overemphasize the value of mental preparedness. Without proper mental preparedness, the best physical conditioning and technical skills will not help you. When danger strikes, uncertainty simmers into anxiety, which boils into panic. Your panic is your assailant's ally. Thus, at the risk of being redundant, we repeat: This vicious chain of events can only be prevented by imagining yourself in as many dangerous situations as is possible. Imagine where to hit, how to hit, and with what to hit.

We are frequently asked by women, "If I master the Conroy Method and am attacked, can you assure me that I'll stay cool and will not panic?" Our answer to this question is "No." Anyone whose life or health is threatened will feel scared—that's to be expected. At first, you may be so terrified that you can't move or think. That's okay. Such reactions usually last only a few seconds or a minute. This is not the time to do anything. As you begin to recover from the shock of being threatened, your mental preparedness will come to your aid. The calmer you become, the easier it will be to plan proper strategies and choose correct tactics. Such thoughts in turn will make you feel calmer. Follow the advice on the label of your mayonnaise jar: "Keep cool, don't freeze." We must stress again, however, that it is perfectly normal to feel frightened, even terrified, when you are first aware that you are in danger.

Never react until you can react properly. To illustrate these points that everyone will be terrified and that you should never react until you can react properly, here is an experience that happened to a former student. She related it to us this way.

> It was about three A.M. on a typical, warm California night. My doors and my bedroom window were closed and locked; the air conditioner was on, and I fell asleep feeling secure. Suddenly I awoke, realized a man was standing by my bed, felt my heart pound, lost my breath, and was paralyzed with fear. He tore the covers off my bed, ripped my nightgown down the front and said if I screamed he'd kill me. As I lay transfixed with fear he undressed and fell on top of me. It could have been the shock of his weight or the filthy language he used, but something clicked in my head and I began to think. First, I realized that he was trying to rape me in my own bed. I began to get angry. Second, I realized that he had no weapon. Only then did I remember what I had learned about fighting. That thought made me calmer, and I began to think of ways of attacking him. I relaxed my body, and soon he freed my arms. Two vulnerable areas were easy for me to reach— his eyes and his groin. I screamed and forcefully gouged both thumbs into his eyes. He fell off me in pain, clutching his eyes. I followed through with a groin pull, and he rolled onto the floor. Next, I kicked him in the head and raced out the door screaming "fire, fire, fire."

Your Seven Tactics

After much research of self-defense literature, talking to our students and readers, and interviewing victims and assailants, we have concluded that the Conroy Method requires only seven basic tactics. We are aware that others advise women to learn dozens of maneuvers that are impractical, many of which call for great athletic skill and continued practice. The seven tactics in the Conroy Method are simple to learn, easy to use, and require no special athletic ability. We can assure you that your self-confidence will increase as you learn these seven tactics and become familiar with their use.

The seven tactics we recommend are listed in order of their importance and usefulness. Each will be described in more detail later.

1. Thumb gouge to the eyes: your best tactic because it is the most effective way to immobilize an assailant.
2. Groin pull: if accessible, your second best means of counterattack.
3. Finger jab to the eyes: not as easy or accurate as the thumb gouge but just as effective.
4. Knee blow to the groin: an effective means of incapacitating an assailant but has limited possibilities for use.
5. Double-hand blow to the neck: a secondary or follow-through technique.
6. Kicks: generally a secondary technique used to force an assailant to the ground. They are especially useful for following through once the assailant is downed. However, kicks are difficult to perform and hard to direct accurately.
7. Screaming: a loud, piercing yell always accompanying your counterattack.

Screams

Begin every counterattack with a scream. Believe it or not, a vicious yell can unnerve even the most determined or irrational assailant. It can also alert someone within earshot to the fact that you are in trouble. Scream from your diaphragm rather than your throat. After all, you want to sound like King Kong, not Minnie Mouse. Take a deep breath and yell "ahhhhhhhhh!" Never yell "help." This places you on the defensive; that is, your assailant will think that you are panicked and that you need help. Even worse, you may then feel that you need help.

An interesting study conducted in New York City several years ago demonstrates a startling reason why yelling "help" is unwise. One evening at about seven P.M., a young woman ran down a dimly lighted street yelling "help, help, help." In this simulated attack, she was chased by a menacing-looking man. Amazingly enough, apartment-house lights went out, blinds were closed, and no one contacted the police. Two weeks later the same woman raced down the same street followed by the same man. This time, however, she yelled "fire, fire, fire." The citizen reaction was reversed. Lights blazed, blinds went up, people appeared at doors and windows, and both the police and fire departments were notified. Moral: When you are running from danger, yell "fire"—not "help."

If you cannot easily scream, practice. We recommend that you practice in your car while driving (with the windows up) or in your home (into a pillow). Your facial expression is also important. Wrinkle your nose, squint your eyes, open your mouth widely, and show your teeth. The more ferocious you can look, the better.

Knowing when not to scream is important, too. We recommend screaming in only three situations. When you are counterattacking, yell "ahhh." When running from an assailant whom you know you can out-distance, yell "fire." After immobilizing an assailant, yell "fire" as you run to safety. In all other circumstances, don't scream. Screaming may aggravate an assailant and encourage him to silence you.

Thumb Gouge

This is your number one tactic—the best weapon you have to in-capacitate an assailant and save your life or health. Once you have de-termined that you can and must fight and if both your hands are free, always use a thumb gouge. An assailant's eyes are the most vulnerable part of his body, exquisitely sensitive to pain, and any injury to them will likely terrify him. A firm thumb gouge will cause temporary or permanent blindness, thus helping you to escape without pursuit.

To deliver a thumb gouge, grasp your assailant's head firmly be-tween both hands with your palms against his ears. (See Figure 4–1.) Force-fully plunge your thumbs into his eyes. If he is wearing glasses, your technique is the same. (See Figure 4–2.)

A thumb gouge is most effectively delivered when an assailant is choking you from your front or sides with his hands. It can also be used from any direction if he has a rope, a tie, a similar weapon around your neck (see Figures 4–3 and 4–4), is ripping your clothes off, and even if he is lying on top of you or sitting next to you. As long as both your hands are free your best weapons are your thumbs, and you should never hesitate to save your life or health by using them.

Some women find it difficult to imagine gouging someone's eyes. They ask such naive questions as "Won't it pop his eyes out?" "Won't it make him bleed all over my hands?" "Will it make me sick to my stomach and unable to follow through with the attack?" To these students, we answer simply and directly as follows: First, you won't be fighting back unless you actually need to immobilize an assailant and flee. Second, eyes may rupture and bleed. Third, mental preparedness will make you realize that your assailant's reactions to pain and blindness are the very things that permit you to escape. Getting sick to your stomach would be a small price to pay for saving your life. Keep in mind, however, that the thumb gouge can inflict permanent damage to an assailant and must be used only when mature judgment dictates.

A gouge to the eyes can be delivered when you are behind an assailant. This simple technique might well have saved a woman, whom we interviewed recently, from being gang raped. While walking to her car at the Los Angeles International Airport parking garage she was accosted by a man with an ice pick who forced her into the back seat of his two-door car. As he began to drive, she took off her shoe, intending to hit him over the head with it. He said, "If you hit me with that shoe, I'll kill you." She remained cowered while he drove her to an apartment in downtown Los Angeles where he and twelve of his accomplices multiple raped her for six hours.

FIG. 4-1
THUMB   GOUGE

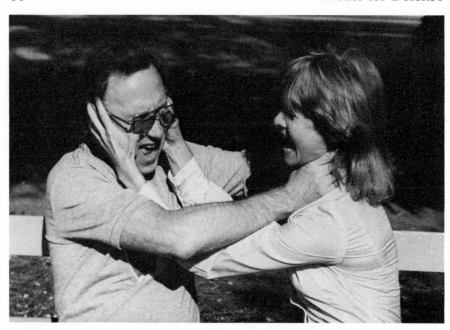

FIG. 4-2 THUMB GOUGE WITH GLASSES

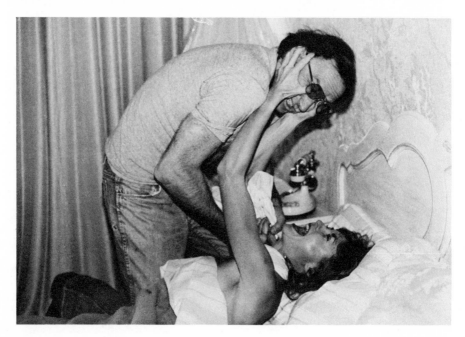

FIG. 4-3 THUMB GOUGE FROM STRANGULATION
WITH OBJECT—SUPINE POSITION

FIG. 4-4a, 4-4b, 4-4c
THUMB GOUGE FROM STRANGULATION WITH OBJECT

FIG. 4-5 EYE GOUGE FROM REAR

When discussing the situation with her, we asked if she thought there was anything she could have done before reaching the apartment to defend herself. She said, "No, there was nothing I could have done." We then asked if while in the back seat of the car she could have administered an eye gouge from the rear. "No!" she said. "That's ridiculous. In the first place, I was behind him and couldn't see his eyes. Second, he was driving fifty miles an hour. I was scared of causing an accident."

In our opinion, this woman was psychologically unprepared. She did not think through the potential danger she was in, nor did she know the proper tactics to use. Had she been aware that an eye gouge from the rear was both possible and easy to administer, she could have waited until he had stopped at a light or stop sign. Then, with a piercing scream she could have swiftly reached forward from behind and dug her middle fingers into his eyes before fleeing the car to safety.

The eye gouge from the rear also can be used under other seemingly difficult situations. For example, if you suddenly came up behind an assailant who was attacking your child, a scream and an eye gouge from the rear could prove lifesaving.

The eye gouge from the rear is done by grasping the assailant's head firmly between your palms and pressing your middle fingers into the eyes. Practicing this maneuver with another person is crucial because you cannot see your target and it is acccomplished entirely by feel. (See Figure 4-5.) If an assailant is wearing glasses, your technique is the same.

In our clinics we encourage students to think of as many ways to use a thumb gouge as they can. They come up with imaginative circumstances such as when swimming, riding in a car, sitting at a bus stop, or even when being suffocated with a pillow. When we practice with a pillow, invariably the student victim is able to gouge the eyes of the would-be attacker even though her face is covered. This is due to the fact that once you have touched someone's head or face, you can locate his eyes instinctively without having to see them. We urge you to try this technique with a friend and a pillow. Be sure to practice in slow motion so that no one is hurt. (See Figure 4-6.)

FIG. 4-6 THUMB GOUGE AGAINST SUFFOCATION ATTACK

Groin Pull

The second major tactic that you must learn is simple, effective, and efficient. The groin pull is simple because the only action required is a squeeze, a twist, and a pull. It is effective because it will instantly force a burly tower of power to the ground, crying with pain. It is efficient because with only one free hand you can easily grab your target from a variety of positions. The most likely positions for starting this counterattack are from a single-wrist grasp, a front or rear bear hug, or a prone, or supine, position with your assailant sitting or lying on you. To execute the groin pull, simply reach your hand between your assailant's legs—the area called the groin—grab his testicles, squeeze, twist, and pull. (See Figure 4-7.)

FIG. 4-7
GROIN PULL

One woman naively wrote, "Are you telling us to grab his penis?" Our answer was, "No, pulling the penis will not incapacitate a man." Another reader inquired, "Won't his penis be in the way?" Our answer was, "Not if the groin pull is performed correctly." As mentioned in the previous paragraph, the groin pull begins by reaching up between the man's legs and grasping his testicles. To avoid telegraphing this maneuver, all groping motions must be eliminated. Once your hand has moved upward so that you feel the testicles and they are in the palm of your hand, squeeze them as hard as you can. Pulling and twisting them at the same time inflicts additional injury. If you do not start pulling and squeezing until you have them firmly in your hand, you will eliminate the possibility of missing. There are no words we can use to describe to a woman the paralyzing pain that this maneuver causes a man. The pain is so deep and intense that the man will double over, may vomit, and even become unconscious for several minutes. Upon regaining consciousness he will still be immobilized for a period of time, certainly long enough for you to follow through with other techniques and flee to safety.

There is one circumstance that prevents a groin pull from being effective, and that is when a man is wearing very tight pants. If this is the case, you can either wait until he removes his pants or execute a finger jab to the eyes—a technique described next in this chapter.

The technique of delaying your counterattack until you can react properly was exemplified by a woman who recently attended one of our lectures. During the question-and-answer period, she stood up and, with grave intensity, challenged our statements about the effectiveness of the groin pull. She said, "You talk about a groin pull. Well, the man who raped me had tight pants on, and there was no way I could have used a groin pull on him." She and the entire audience gave an insightful sigh when we said simply, "Were his pants on during the entire rape?" In a survey that we recently conducted under the auspices of the Los Angeles Police Department, we found that the groin pull is being taught in numerous police academies throughout the country. It is recommended to peace officers because it is an effective weapon for both men and women to use and can temporarily immobilize even the most vicious attacker.

The prohibition for women using the groin pull has an interesting history. The Bible, in Deuteronomy, chapter 25, verse 11, instructs that if a woman aiding her husband who is fighting another man "puts out her hand and catches hold of the man's genitals," she shall have her hand cut off and be shown no mercy.

I (Mary Conroy) recently showed the effectiveness of a groin pull when invited to give a demonstration on a national TV program. The guest celebrity, a six-foot, 220-pound, ex-football player, was very skeptical that "little Mary" could free herself if he attacked her. He as much as said "This self-defense stuff doesn't work." Then, without rehearsal, he forcefully grabbed five-foot four-inch, 104-pound "little Mary" in a tight bear hug from behind. Instinctively I reached for his groin and gave him a tug. He doubled over instantaneously, gasping painfully under his breath, "You can't do that on national television." Really wanting to even the score, I cooed solicitously, "Oh, are you hurt?" "I don't think so," said he, attempting to straighten up, "and you certainly proved your point." Actually, two things can be learned from this story: (1) the groin pull really works, and (2) don't practice it on a man unless you are very gentle or demonstrating the tactic before a television audience.

Practicing the groin pull full force, however, is important, and it's unlikely you'll find a willing subject. Therefore, we suggest (and you're not going to believe this one) that you put two golf balls into a sock and tie it to a doorknob. From various angles, practice reaching up, grabbing, twisting, and pulling the golf balls. This, as you can imagine, is quickly mastered. Next, place the sock and balls in the crotch of a pair of slacks you are wearing. Note the force required to dig your fingers up and into the crotch in order to grasp the balls firmly. If your pants are loose, little force is required. If they are snug, your fingers will hurt a bit when executing the groin pull correctly.

Finger Jab

   A finger jab is your third major tactic and can save your life in the most threatening of situations. We have placed this tactic in the third position because it is less accurate and less forceful than the thumb gouge or groin pull.

   To deliver this blow, hold your wrist, hand, and fingers firmly. The target for the finger jab is the eyes. Start the jab from any position, and forcefully thrust your slightly curved fingers into the assailant's eyes. Jab with all four fingers to increase your chances of contacting his eyes. (See Figure 4–8.) If he is wearing glasses, direct your fingers to his upper cheek, just under the lower rim. Upon striking his cheek, your fingers will naturally continue under the glasses and into his eyes. This blow must be quick, forceful, and accurately aimed. It can cause temporary or permanent blindness.

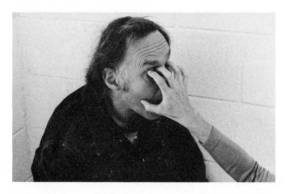

FIG. 4-8
FINGER   JAB

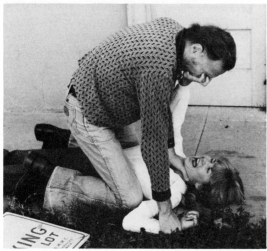

FIG. 4-9
FINGER   JAB   FROM
LYING   POSITION

   Examples of when to use a finger jab are if the assailant is wearing
tight jeans (thus ruling out the groin pull), is holding you by one arm
(thus ruling out the thumb gouge), and is dragging you forcefully to the
edge of a cliff (thus ruling out the possibility of waiting to react or talking
to him). With life and health in immediate danger, a finger jab is your
tactic of choice.
   Another situation in which this tactic could be lifesaving is if an
assailant is lying on top of of you, choking you with one hand, and holding one of your arms down with his other hand. In this situation you only
have one hand free. Since you are being choked, you would not have time
to try and talk or to wait for a better opportunity. A finger jab to the eyes
is your tactic of choice. (See Figure 4–9.) You would also use a finger jab
when an assailant is threatening you with a weapon such as a knife or
gun. With one hand you must block the weapon, and with the free hand
you deliver a finger jab to his vulnerable eyes. (See Figure 5–6 on page
87.)

Knee Lift

   Before describing this and the next three tactics, we wish to emphasize the fact that they are more difficult to employ and have limited
usefulness. For this reason, you should not think of them as your primary
tactics for personal defense but rather as ancillary, or secondary, weapons
in your arsenal. A forceful blow to the groin with your knee can temporarily incapacitate a man. This blow has limited value because it can
only be delivered to an assailant who is standing directly in front of you
and close by. To deliver it, shift your weight to one leg and forcefully
drive your other knee up into the assailant's groin. (See Figure 4–10.) Do
not lean back before delivering this blow, because this may telegraph
your intention. Since this is an obvious form of attack, many men are on
guard for it. In fact, "Knee him in the groin" is a cliché to many.
   One of the rare circumstances in which you might initiate an attack
with a knee lift is when an assailant has confronted you by grasping both
of your forearms and is standing with his legs slightly apart directly in
front of you. In this obvious situation his groin is so easily accessible that
you might consider it as a beginning tactic. However, if you miss his groin
and accidently hit his thigh, you risk infuriating your assailant. Therefore, we repeat that the knee lift is most successfully used as a secondary
attack weapon. After a thumb gouge and while your thumbs are still in his
eyes, driving your knee up and into his groin is an excellent means of
following through.

FIG. 4-10
KNEE LIFT

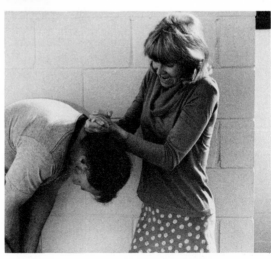

FIG. 4-11
DOUBLE-HAND BLOW
TO THE NECK

Double-Hand Blow

This tactic is to be used only when your assailant is reacting in pain to your primary attack. Thus, it is also a secondary or follow-through maneuver. It is effectively delivered to the back of the neck. For example, if you have executed a groin pull or dislocated his knee with a kick, your assailant will most likely be doubled over with his head down, thus exposing the back of his neck.

A double-hand blow is delivered by joining your hands as if clapping (do not interwine your fingers), bending your elbows, and striking the assailant's neck with the side of your hand as shown in Figure 4–11. The arm motion when striking the back of the neck resembles the motion of chopping wood.

A natural instinct when delivering this blow is to wind up. It is not only unnecessary to begin a blow by winding up, but it is also self-defeating. We are referring to our previous comments about losing the element of surprise by "telegraphing" your intentions. As you practice this tactic, you will be surprised to find how little force is added by winding up.

Blows must be delivered quickly. The principles of physics demonstrate that the force of a blow is dependent on the speed with which it is delivered. For this reason, a small woman delivering a swift blow can cause more pain and injury than a strong, muscle-bound man delivering a moderate blow. Practicing to develop speed is therefore essential in your training. Blows and jabs should be aimed at an imaginary point a few inches behind your actual target.

Kicks

Your legs are the strongest part of your body. Even a slightly built woman can immobilize the largest man with a well-placed kick. Only forty pounds of pressure is necessary to dislocate a knee. Kicking has other advantages. Kicks delivered from a distance keep you out of an assailant's reach. (See Figure 4–12.) Also, most men are not used to blocking kicks and cannot defend themselves. Even men who are experienced boxers do not know how to block a properly executed kick. Kicks are used as a follow-through tactic in almost every form of attack. You should practice until you become a competent kicker.

It is not necessary to wear shoes for a kicking attack. Your bare feet can cause as much damage as the heel of your shoe. If you are wearing high heels, we recommend that you remove them to improve your balance.

Fig. 4-12
LENGTH OF LEGS

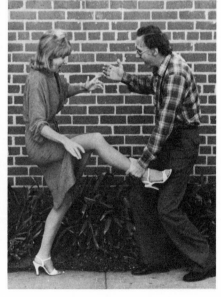

FIG. 4-13
INCORRECT   KICKS

The specific target you choose depends on two factors: (1) what vulnerable areas are exposed and (2) the type of injury you wish to inflict. The most vulnerable areas to kick are your assailant's knee, and when he is on the ground, his face, the side of his head, and his throat. Once you have chosen the area, imagine that your exact target is six to eight inches behind the actual spot. By this we mean that you should aim your kick through your target, not at it. Thus, if the area you want to hit on your assailant is his face, aim through his face to an imaginary spot at the back of his head. This will ensure that your foot strikes with maximum momentum.

Use the heel and the instep of your foot to contact the target. Do not try to use your toes because you could break them. All kicks are delivered without winding up. Curb your natural instinct to swing your leg back before kicking. A backswing "telegraphs" the fact that a kick is on the way. Such warnings eliminate the element of surprise, and your assailant may move or catch your foot. (See Figure 4–13.)

Learning to kick properly is the most difficult tactic we recommend. It requires agility, coordination, and careful aim. In most attack situations, the assailant doesn't cooperate by standing still, and hitting a moving target is very difficult.

Front Kick

A front kick is used when you are facing your assailant. Learn this kick in three steps:

1. Lift your knee toward your chest, flex your foot, and bend your supporting leg slightly.
2. Extend your leg straight out, keeping your foot flexed, and contact the target with your heel and instep, not the ball of your foot or your toes.
3. Flex your leg back to the first position, with your knee still raised. From this position you can kick again if necessary.

After mastering these three steps individually (See Figure 4–14), practice delivering kicks until you can do them so quickly that your foot can hardly be seen. The front kick is delivered to the knee. When kicking the knee, turn your foot slightly inward to afford you more surface-striking area. A front kick could be used if a man is strangling you from the front and holding you at arm's distance. In this unlikely situation a thumb gouge would be impossible, and a front kick is your only possible tactic. (See Figure 4–21.)

FIG. 4-14 FRONT KICK

FIG. 4-15
SIDE KICK

FIG. 4-16
REAR KICK

Side Kick

A side kick is the most accurate and powerful of all kicks. Thus, whenever possible, it should be used in preference to other kicks. Again, learn the kick in three steps:

1. Lift your leg directly sidewards, with the knee well bent and your foot flexed. Simultaneously bend your supporting knee as you lean slightly away from the direction in which you intend to kick. The higher you lift your knee and the further you bend, the higher you will be able to contact a target. For example, when kicking a short assailant's knee, you would not need to raise your knee higher or bend more than a few inches. If he is very tall, you must lift your knee very high and bend very far sideways.
2. Extend your leg out, keeping your foot flexed, and contact the target with your heel and instep.
3. Flex your leg back to the first position and prepare to kick again. It is not necessary to straighten your body or return your foot to the ground between kicks.

Side kicks are aimed at an assailant's closest knee with your closest foot. After you have forced him to the ground, side kicks are also directed to his head and neck. (See Figure 4–19.) The only time a kick should be used as an initial or first tactic is when an eye gouge or groin pull is impossible. This could occur if a man has grabbed both your wrists and is about to force you into his car. (See Figure 4–15.)

Rear Kick

The rear kick is only used when you are attacked from behind because it is very difficult to aim. Learn the rear kick in a series of three movements:

1. Raise the striking foot backward while flexing the ankle. Turn the foot outward to increase the surface area with which you can contact your target. Bend your supporting knee as you lean forward slightly.
2. Kick your leg backward with the ankle flexed, and contact his knee with your heel and instep.
3. Bring your foot back to the starting position so that you are ready to kick again.

Look down at his knee to aim your kick. A kick to the rear is only delivered to the knee. Do not aim for the shin or instep because this will just hurt rather than incapacitate your assailant. Since a rear kick is very difficult to aim and execute, use it only when a groin pull is impossible. A situation in which a rear kick would be necessary is if an assailant grabs you from the rear, holds both of your wrists, and is dragging you toward the edge of a cliff. Since you must react immediately, a rear kick is your only appropriate tactic. (See Figure 4–16.)

One last point concerning kicks. We must stress the importance of your being able to deliver kicks rapidly. Initially, we suggest you learn the kicks in three steps. Once the steps are mastered, practice them with a three-count rhythm. When you can perform this smoothly, speed up the rhythm until you can do the entire kick in one smooth motion and so fast that the eye cannot follow. The ultimate force delivered by your kick depends more on its speed than the strength behind it. Become proficient in kicking with both legs because you never know in advance which one you will have to use.

Knee Break

This tactic is used when no help is near. It ensures the immobility of your assailant. After rendering him unconscious with a gouge, blows, and kicks, roll him onto his back, pick up his leg securely in both hands, and stamp forcefully through the knee. (See Figure 4–17.)

The Conroy Method

The Conroy Method of Self-defense is simple. You learn to be safe by being prepared, by getting out of situations before they become dangerous, and—when threatened—by inflicting injury, immobilizing your assailant, and fleeing to safety. Fancy fighting techniques and fancy weapons are not practical for the average woman, and we don't recommend them. As the Conroy Method evolved (and we constantly work to improve it), we have become convinced that it works best when women rely on only seven simple tactics. We used to teach over twenty techniques. These included a hand blow to the nose, a groin hit, a kick to the groin, and a host of releases and takedowns. While useful in practiced hands or as part of martial-arts courses, they are difficult and unnecessary. Unless you have black-belt proficiency, attempting complicated releases, takedowns, and throws could increase your danger rather than help you escape. A release easily accomplished in the safe and sterile environment of the classroom may not work in a dirty alley, and even if a takedown did work, you might be faced with an assailant whose only injury is to his ego. But with less effort and skill, an eye gouge or groin pull could paralyze him with pain and allow you time to flee.

FIG. 4-17 KNEE BREAK

Maneuvers

When you are confronted with a situation in which you are grabbed without warning, your first concern, if possible, is to find out what the assailant wants and comply if you can. If you cannot comply and feel that your life or health is in danger, use the following techniques.

1. Begin each counterattack with a fierce scream—"Ahhh."
2. Execute eye gouges, groin pulls, blows, and kicks until the assailant is down.
3. Continue kicking until he is totally incapacitated.
4. Run, screaming "fire, fire."
5. Contact the police.

The following maneuvers describe possible tactics for gaining your freedom. They are not combinations that must always be performed in a specific order. Use them only as suggestions, and then mentally create your own combinations of tactics.

Single-Wrist Maneuver

Situation: An assailant grabs your left wrist with both of his hands.

Tactic: If he pulls you toward the bushes or a car, do not pull against him. Go with him a few steps to gain your balance. Then scream and deliver a groin pull or, if he is wearing tight pants, a finger jab with your free hand. (See Figure 4–18.) Follow through with a double-hand blow, kicks, and run, screaming "fire, fire." Your technique is the same if the assailant grabs your wrist with only one hand.

FIG. 4-18   SINGLE-WRIST MANEUVER

Double-Wrist Maneuver

Situation: An assailant grabs both your wrists with his hands.

Tactic: Scream and deliver a knee to the groin. As he releases your hands, clasp them together for a double-hand blow to the back of his neck. Follow through with kicks and run screaming "fire, fire." (See Figure 4–19.)

FIG. 4-19
DOUBLE-WRIST MANEUVER

Front-Choke Maneuver

Situation: An assailant standing in front of you is strangling you with both hands or a scarf or a necktie.

Tactic 1: Bent-arm choke. If you are being held close enough to reach your assailant's eyes, scream and deliver a thumb gouge to his eyes. With your thumbs still in his eyes, follow through with a knee to his groin, and as he doubles over deliver a double-hand blow to the back of his neck. Continue your counterattack with kicks and run screaming "fire, fire." (See Figure 4–20.)

FIG. 4-20
FRONT-CHOKE MANEUVER. TACTIC 1: BENT-ARM CHOKE

Tactic 2: Straight-arm choke. It is unlikely that an assailant would choke you at arm's length so that you could not reach his eyes. But if he does and you cannot reach his eyes with your hands, dislocate his knee with a front kick. (See Figure 4–21.) As this occurs, step foward and gouge your thumbs into his eyes. If your windpipe is pressed, you will have only seconds to react before blacking out. Therefore act quickly and remember —when a man attempts to strangle you, your life is at stake. The most vicious defense is thus warranted.

*FIG. 4-21
FRONT-CHOKE
MANEUVER.
TACTIC 2:
STRAIGHT-ARM CHOKE*

Rear-Choke Maneuver

Situation: An assailant grabs your throat from behind with both hands. *Tactic:* Scream, glance downward and back to locate your target, and deliver a groin pull or, if he is wearng tight pants, a rear kick to his knee. When his grip loosens, turn and deliver a thumb gouge to his eyes, a knee in his groin, continue with kicks, and run screaming "fire, fire." (See Figure 4–22.)

Unlike the situation in which you are strangled from the rear with a necktie, nylon stocking, or rope and can simply turn to execute a thumb gouge, when a man's hands are holding you by the neck from the rear, you cannot turn around. Therefore your only possible initial tactic is a groin pull or, if the assailant is wearing tight pants, a rear kick.

FIG. 4-22
REAR-CHOKE
MANEUVER

Hair Maneuver

Situation: An assailant grabs your hair. *Tactic:* Do not attempt to pull away from him because this will hurt and you could lose a handful of hair. Instead, move toward him a few steps to keep your balance, scream, deliver a thumb gouge or, if he is also holding one hand, a groin pull or finger jab, follow through with a double-hand blow, kicks, and run screaming "fire, fire." (See Figure 4–23.)

FIG. 4-23
HAIR MANEUVER

FIG. 4-23b (CONT'D)

Ground Maneuver

Situation: An assailant throws you to the ground and leaps on top of you. *Tactic 1: Sitting-position release.* When you are thrown to the ground, leap to your feet, if possible. If, however, the assailant pounces on top of you, here is how to free yourself: (1) Scream and injure him by executing a thumb gouge, groin pull, or finger jab. (2) After he is injured, it will be easy to roll him off you by shoving his upper body to your right or left. (3) As soon as he is off your body, leap to your feet and deliver kicks to his head and neck. (4) When you are certain that he is immobilized, run screaming "fire, fire." (See Figure 4–24.)

Tactic 2: Lying-position release. If an assailant is lying on top of you, scream as you execute a thumb gouge, finger jab, or, if possible, a groin pull. Roll him off your body by placing your hands under his shoulders and shoving him to the side. Leap to your feet and deliver kicks to his head and neck. (See Figure 4–25.)

Unconventional Maneuvers

Since it is impossible to describe every way in which an assailant could grab you, it should be comforting to know that once you are familiar with the maneuvers described above, you will be able to free yourself from practically any hold. Just scream, use your best available tactics, aim at his vulnerable targets, and try to keep your wits about you.

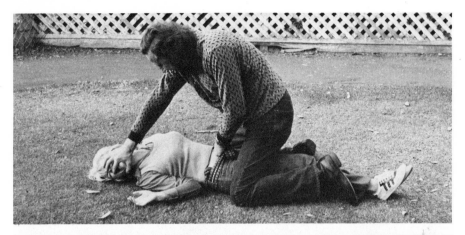

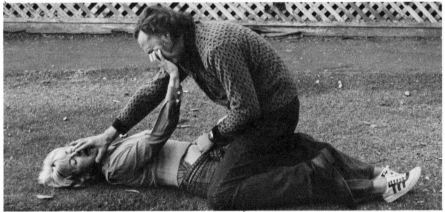

FIG. 4-24
GROUND MANEUVER. TACTIC 1: SITTING POSITION

FIG. 4-24
GROUND MANEUVER. TACTIC 1: SITTING POSITION (CONT'D)

Double-Knee Drop

This technique requires little practice and is rarely used. For this reason, it is not listed as one of your seven tactics. It should only be used if help is far away because it could paralyze your assailant. After rendering him unconscious with gouges, kicks, and blows, roll him onto his stomach and drop heavily with both your knees on the small of his back. (See Figure 4–26.)

FIG. 4-25
GROUND MANEUVER. TACTIC 2: LYING-POSITION RELEASE

FIG. 4-26   DOUBLE-KNEE DROP

Summary

The tactics we have described in this chapter can be easily learned and applied by all women. Our experience, however, repeatedly has shown that certain people have greater difficulty mastering certain skills. Therefore, we recommend that you emphasize in your practice sessions those techniques that seem the most awkward or difficult. Practice and patience make perfect—and the skills you are mastering may prove life-saving.

Chapter 5
Weapons

We strongly recommend that you learn to protect yourself by using your five natural body weapons—your voice, fingers and thumbs, hands, knees, and legs. Natural weapons are easily aimed and, of course, are always with you. No assailant can take them from you and use them against you. They enable you to maintain your element of surprise and, most importantly, your confidence is in yourself, not in your can of Mace, keys, or other purse weapons. Some women, however, prefer to use purse weapons, and thus we include techniques on their use.

You should keep in mind the following difficulties involved in relying on them. Vanity itself can interfere. Would you walk through a parking lot with a can of Mace in one hand and a bundle of Christmas presents in the other? Wouldn't you feel silly standing at a bus stop with books in one hand and tear gas in the other? Overcoming such embarrassment is necessary because, as the manufacturers of these products tell you, they must be in your hand at all times to be effective. The few precious seconds required to fish a Mace can out of your purse, aim it, and press the button would warn an assailant of your counterattack, infuriate him, and give him time to strike you. In addition, if you have time to search your purse, you should spend it running and yelling "fire, fire."

Another problem in relying on Mace for protection is that it may offer a false sense of security, even if you have it in your hand. The ineffectiveness of tear gas was demonstrated on the NBC television consumer-affairs program "Fightback" with David Horowitz. At close range Mr. Horowitz sprayed the face of a certified tear-gas instructor. It took over fifteen seconds for the instructor to feel the effect. During that time he had stolen Mr. Horowitz's wallet and watch. In an actual situation, the robber would not be so courteous. After being sprayed with tear gas, most assailants would be infuriated and retaliate with physical assault.

A second example of how tear gas can offer a false sense of security was illustrated by Judy Ravits, executive director of the Los Angeles County Commission on Assaults Against Women. After exposing herself to a direct spray of tear gas, she reported that it took as long as forty-five seconds for a reaction. "My eyes started to burn and my nose started to run. The sting was not as much as a bee sting." Within seconds she was able to read and do jumping jacks. The Los Angeles Commission on the Status of Women no longer endorses the use of tear gas.

A third example of the ineffectiveness of tear gas was demonstrated by one of our students who argued in its favor. She produced a can that she had been carrying for several months. When she was asked to demonstrate it for the class, we were astonished when it failed to work because it had no pressure. Or, can you imagine sleeping with a Mace can in your hand? One student reported to the class that she used to keep a can of Mace under her pillow. She said "used to" because one night she awoke gagging when her trusty Mace can leaked.

Carrying any purse weapon may alert an assailant to your intentions. We call that "telegraphing." We can easily imagine an assailant stalking a victim, seeing her weapon, and grabbing it. This leaves the victim defenseless because she counted on her purse weapon for protection. Enraged, he now uses it on her. But if she had relied on her body for protection and he grabbed one hand, she would still have a second hand. Or if he grabbed both hands, she would have her knees and legs to fight with. Fighting with your body offers options. Purse weapons do not.

Every month the Ogden City P.T.A. invites a guest speaker to discuss contemporary issues. Recently a self-defense expert taught the group how to use handbag items for defense. Since hearing the speaker, Linda—along with many other women—has been carrying a small can of hair spray for protection.

It was 6:30 P.M. and Linda was leaving work. Most of the other employees had already gone, and as she walked to her car, she sensed that someone was behind her. Linda's intuition was correct, and so she slid her hand into her purse and pulled out the hair spray. Suddenly a man grasped her upper arm. She held her weapon out and pressed her finger down on the nozzle. The man, eyes burning and enraged, thrust his fist into Linda's face. The hairspray hurt Linda's assailant. It did not incapacitate him, and instead, he incapacitated her.

To further demonstrate the point, let's examine Mildred's situation. Mildred was always a cautious woman. She lived on the tenth floor of a secure apartment building. She installed double-cylinder dead-bolt locks on her doors and never went out alone in the evening. In a leading women's magazine, Mildred discovered an article on self-defense that recommended using a hat pin to ward off assailants. She was so inspired by the suggestion that she went to the dime store and purchased a four-inch-long hat pin.

One Sunday after church, she stepped into her elevator and pushed the button for the tenth floor. As the door closed, a man hurried in. They rode in silence for three floors. Suddenly the man jammed his thumb into the stop button. "Give me your money, lady." Horrified, she handed him her handbag. "Now the ring," he commanded. Mildred hesitated, since the ring was the only remembrance she had of her late husband. She reached up, pulled the hat pin from her bonnet, and jabbed it into the man's stomach. "Why, you bitch!" he screamed as his fist smashed down across Mildred's terrified face. He angrily jerked the ring off her finger, released the stop button, and leaped off the elevator at the next floor.

Mildred was lucky. The consequences suffered by her could have been disastrous—even fatal.

In all of the examples above, our hapless victims relied on things that could be taken away from them rather than on natural weapons (voice, fingers and thumbs, hands, knees, and legs). This is the very reason why the Conroy Method does not endorse a personal defense product. Whenever we are requested to do so, we ask the promoter (who is always male): "Do you carry this product for yourself?" Invariably the response, beginning with a chuckle, is "No, my product is for women." When we ask "What would you do if you were attacked?" the answer is "I'd slug the guy." We reply, "Why shouldn't a woman protect herself that way too?" "Oh, women can't fight. They need an equalizer." This type of male chauvinistic ignorance unfortunately has convinced many women that they can't effectively use their body weapons. Thus brainwashed, a woman will trust gadgets rather than her body. It seems a travesty to suggest to women that in order to secure their own protection they must carry something in their hands for the rest of their lives.

Despite our recommendations against the use of purse weapons, many students and self-defense teachers demand some pointers in their use. For these women we supply the following information concerning the use of purses, books, umbrellas, and so on. Women who feel comfortable using their natural weapons can disregard this advice and proceed to the section entitled Defense Against Assailant's Weapons on page 86.

Weapons for Defense

Mental preparedness and quick-wittedness can allow you to change innocent purse objects into handy weapons or shields. Because an assailant could readily take your gun, switchblade knife, or blackjack and use it against you, we do not recommend carrying such weapons. We even extend this advice a step further: Never use a kitchen knife, a razor blade, a fingernail file, or a pair of scissors against an assailant.

When the Hillside Strangler was killing at will, women in the Los Angeles area were living in terror. A local television station asked us to conduct an informal survey to determine how women were preparing to defend themselves. When we stopped women at random on the street, we were shocked and concerned by our discoveries. Several women were carrying knives or scissors in ther purses. "What will you do with your weapon if you are attacked?" We questioned. "I'll stab the guy," they would respond bravely. "Where will you stab him?" we would continue. A look of astonishment would appear on their faces. "Well, I don't know . . . anywhere. Maybe the chest?" Clearly, one should not aim "anywhere." A woman probably would have just one opportunity to thrust a knife into an assailant. If it doesn't kill him instantly (which is highly unlikely), he will take it from her and use it on her (which is highly likely).

Several other women we interviewed had recently purchased handguns at their local sporting-goods stores. Although they had received no training and had never fired the weapons, they were staking their lives on them.

Mrs. Anne Sebree of Tomball, Texas, knew how to use her .38 pistol. Early one July morning in 1978, at about 4:30, she heard noises, grabbed her weapon, and, in the dark, fired into the face of a man, killing him. The man was her twenty-seven-year-old son, Earl, who had just arrived from Oklahoma City to plan a surprise party for his mother's sixty-eighth birthday. Need we say more?

Each of the following defense tactics described in this section is initiated with screams and concluded with kicks to an assailant's knees and, once he has fallen to the ground, his head and neck.

Noisemaker

A scream is the best noisemaker you can use. For those women who have difficulty screaming, we recommend carrying a compressed air siren or a gymnasium whistle. A siren is better because when you turn it on it will continue to emit a piercing, shrill sound as long as you need it. A whistle must be held in your mouth and blown, which is often difficult to do when you are frightened. Blow your whistle in a long–short–short signal, and the asssailant may believe you are a policewoman. Under no circumstances should you wear a noisemaker around your neck by a cord. An assailant could attempt to strangle you with this cord. Instead, keep the noisemaker handy on your key chain or in your pocket.

Purse

To use your purse as a weapon, hold it in both hands, point the most rigid portion at your assailant, and jab it up under his nose or into his throat. (See Figure 5–1.) Most purses are large enough to serve as a shield against a knife. Grasp your purse firmly in both hands, and use it to block knife thrusts as you kick into your assailant's knee.

Book or Package

A book or a package can be used in a manner similar to your purse. When using one as a weapon, aim the sharpest edge toward your assailant's nose or into his throat.

FIG. 5-1
USING A PURSE AS A WEAPON.

Newspaper or Magazine

A rolled newspaper or magazine can be used as a weapon. It is best to jab the end of the rolled newspaper or magazine into your assailant's throat or up under his nose. Curb your natural instinct to swat or slap at the assailant, because such blows cannot inflict much damage and are easily blocked. (See Figure 5–2.)

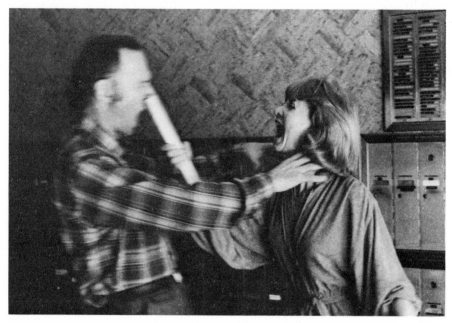

FIG. 5-2   USING A NEWSPAPER AS A WEAPON.

Flashlight

A flashlight can become a weapon when jabbed, end first, into an assailant's neck or nose. Again, you must resist your natural instinct to swat or swing it sideways.

Keys

Keys can be used as weapons. It is important to hold them a special way so that when they strike your target they do not slip from your grip. Grasp them in the palm of your hand and have the sharp end of each key protrude between your fingers. Hard jabs into the eyes and throat are most effective. It takes time to arrange keys properly, and so if you plan to use them for self-defense it is best to hold them as described while walking in potentially dangerous areas. (See Figure 5-3.)

Umbrella, Broomstick, or Mop Handle

Long, slender objects can be used in one of two ways. *As a shield:* Grasp the shaft with your hands, spread your hands about two feet apart, and hold the object parallel to the floor in front of you. If the assailant grabs it, allow him to pull you close enough to kick into his knees (Figure 5–4). *As a spear:* Hold the shaft at the side of your body with your hands ten to twelve inches apart, and point the sharp end at your assailant. Direct jabs into his groin or throat. If he grasps the point, simply let him pull you toward him, and kick into his knees.

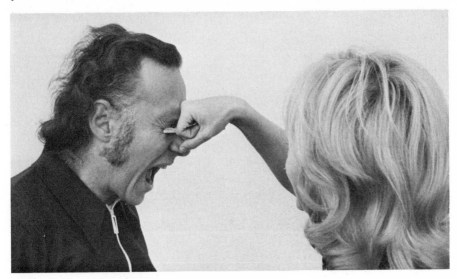

FIG. 5-3.   USING KEYS AS A WEAPON.

FIG. 5-4
USING A BROOM
AS A WEAPON.

Pen or Pencil

Once again, we recommend that you use your thumbs and fingers as weapons in preference to a pen or pencil. However if the thought of physical contact with an assailant really inhibits you, a handy pen or pencil may be more psychologically acceptable.

Hold it firmly in your hand, and jab the sharp end into the assailant's eyes. (See Figure 5–5.)

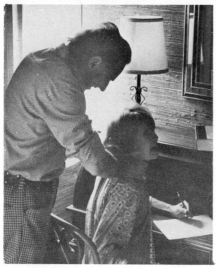

FIG. 5-5
USING A PENCIL AS A WEAPON.

Purse Contents

Combs, brushes, and lipstick cases—typical items carried in a purse —may not be as handy or effective as one might think. Contrary to the opinions of some experts, we caution against their use. Not only are they difficult to get at, hold, and strike with, but they are far less effective than your fingers or hands.

Tear Gas

In many states the use of tear gas by civilians is illegal. In several states citizens can participate in a tear-gas class and acquire certification to carry it. In a few states tear gas can be purchased through mail-order houses or in hardware stores. Check with your local police department before purchasing it. Tear gas is a liquid contained in a canister twice the size of a lipstick. The promoters of tear gas recommend carrying it in your hand, on your key chain or attached to your belt or purse for easy access. Tear gas is emitted in a stream. When contact is made with the skin, a burning sensation takes place. Eyes water and breathing becomes difficult. While we do not recommend its use, we do suggest if you use tear gas that you be prepared to run and scream "fire" immediately. Don't hang around to see if it works. The effects of tear gas are neither permanent nor lethal. We caution you that tear gas is not discriminating. If you are downwind of your assailant, you may wind up more teary-eyed than he.

Commercially Available Self-defense Items

Because of the crime waves sweeping our cities, stores are filled with items advertised as "ultimate self-defense weapons." Despite the fact that many of these weapons are illegal and have been proved ineffective by law-enforcement agents, they continue to be widely advertised and recommended by so-called experts. For example, you can still purchase electric-shock sticks. If a shock stick is to work properly, two electrodes must be in direct contact with a victim's skin and the "on" button has to be pressed at the crucial moment. Thick clothing can block the current and render the stick useless.

In conclusion, we do not recommend that you purchase gadgets. Nothing you can buy, take from your purse, or pick up at home is more effective than your voice, fingers and thumbs, hands, knees, and legs. To reiterate, your body weapons are always available, easy to aim, simple to use, cannot be taken away from you or used against you, and guard your element of surprise. Moreover, your confidence is in you, not in a gadget.

Defense Against an Assailant's Weapons

It is well known that many assailants use weapons simply to frighten people and get their cooperation. However, as newspapers report daily, threats of violence all too often are carried out. Your general strategy for personal defense is: Always cooperate with an armed assailant. Try to be calm, find out what he wants, and if he demands your valuables, give them to him quickly. In every way try to avoid a physical confrontation. **The tactics we are about to describe should only be used in life-threatening situations.**

How will you know whether an assailant is just intimidating you or actually intending to kill you? There is no definitive answer to this question, but certain guidelines can be followed to help you determine the seriousness of a threat. If an assailant acts in a grossly irrational manner, his threats must be taken very seriously. By contrast, a professional robber will make his demands plain and be as eager to get away as you are to have him leave. A psychotic individual who is acting on the basis of delusions will force you to act according to his demented schemes. For example, a psychotic assailant will often tell his victim to say things, to act a part, or to go to a specific place where he can re-create his fantasy. Another type of psychotic individual who frequently attacks women is a drug addict. While under the influence of the drug or in the midst of a withdrawal reaction, he is easy to recognize. Addicts have sudden mood changes and may show poor coordination. When in a withdrawal phase, they may show evidence of physical pain, poor coordination, and severe agitation (shaking of the hands and legs). They may also sweat profusely and talk rapidly and irrationally.

Once you decide that you must physically defend yourself against an armed assailant, remember that your decision is based on your feeling that you are about to be seriously injured or murdered. A complete, all-out attack is warranted. Killing an assailant in self-defense is justified both morally and legally.

Defense Against a Knife Attack

Your first tactic when defending yourself against an assailant armed with a knife is to maintain your distance. Run and scream "fire, fire" whenever there is a good chance that you can escape. If he is within arm's reach and you cannot run, try to talk your way out of having to fight by finding out what he wants and complying if you can.

If you are about to be stabbed, you must use the following tactics. If the knife is pointed at the left side of your body, scream as you thrust your right hand across your body, with your thumb down, and grasp his wrist firmly to force it aside. Do not attempt to pin his arm, because this may well be impossible. Rather, block it away as you deliver a finger jab to his eyes with your free hand (Figure 5–6). If he is still clutching the knife, do not try to take it away. Instead, run screaming "fire, fire." If he drops it, kick it away, and continue your attack until he is totally immobilized. Reverse the technique if his knife is pointing at the right side of your body by thrusting his wrist out with your left hand. Never try to pick up his knife, and never attempt to stab him with it.

Even if your assailant manages to slash or puncture you, you should fight. This is particularly important because rarely is a victim incapacitated by one knife wound. A superficial knife wound may cause profuse bleeding and frighten you into stopping your attack when you could still incapacitate the assailant. A recent news item in the *Los Angeles Times* proved this point. It related how twenty-seven-year-old Gwendolyn Rose was stabbed over thirty times and lived to tell the tale. If you are stabbed, don't attempt to block his blows. Rather, immediately execute a thumb gouge to your assailant's eyes.

 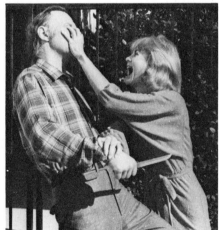

FIG. 5-6 DEFENSE AGAINST A KNIFE.

Knives are often used by rapists. If a rapist is using a knife only to frighten you, there is a very good chance that he will put it down when you are sufficiently passive. Thus, waiting and pretending to cooperate may create the opportunity to fight him unarmed. (See Figure 5–7.) This advice is based upon interviews with hundreds of rape victims who told us that their assailants put down their knives just before or during the course of their rapes.

Rapists have also confirmed that they use weapons only to intimidate their victims into submission. One paroled rapist we interviewed in class was asked the question "Did you use a weapon with the woman you raped?" He thought for a moment, gave a hoarse laugh, and replied,"I used the knife to scare the _____ out of her, and when I knew she'd go along with it, I put the knife down 'cause I didn't need it anymore. I couldn't have held it at her throat all the time I was doing it. What do you think I am, some kind of octopus?" Your chances are excellent that if you are patient your assailant will disarm himself, thus providing you with the opportunity to fight. Remember: Wait until you can react properly, and then fight.

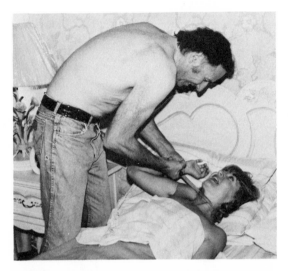

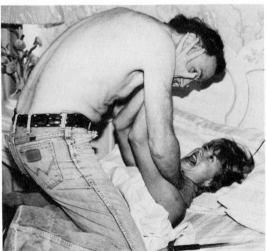

FIG. 5-7
RAPE DEFENSE
AGAINST A KNIFE.

Gun Attack

Never, we repeat, never fight an assailant who has a gun unless you are certain that he intends to shoot you. The reason for this advice is that any defense against a gun-wielding assailant may not work. Therefore, you should always cooperate fully when a gun is pointed at you. As in the case of a knife-wielding rapist, there is a strong likelihood that a man with a gun will disarm himself just before or during the sexual part of his assault. Waiting for this opportunity to fight and preserving your element of surprise are crucial tactics that can save your life. By mentally preparing yourself and waiting for the gun to be put down, you will be able to seize an opportunity that you might not have known existed. One victim told us "a gun was held on me continuously for seven hours while I was raped five times." This indeed was how it appeared to her. But on closer questioning, she unwittingly revealed that while she was "being raped in the bedroom" her assailant "placed the gun on the bedstand during intercourse," "had gone into a bathroom to use the toilet," and "had gone to the kitchen to make himself a sandwich." Her terror did not allow her to recognize that the gun was not aimed at her the entire time.

It is not uncommon for an assailant to threaten by illusion, as illustrated by the true story of a young woman we interviewed while lecturing in Chicago. She sobbingly related being forced into the back seat of an acquaintence's car and then raped. "How long did the rape take?" "About forty-five minutes" was her reply. "How did he force you into the back seat?" "He had a gun," she said convincingly. "What kind of gun was it?" we questioned. Hesitatingly she said, "I don't know." "What did it look like?" we persisted. She sobbed again and blurted out, "Well, I didn't actually see it. He said it was in the glove compartment. I know it was there, I just know it." As implausible as this story seems, remember that to an unprepared person the threat of being murdered leads to panic and irrational behavior.

If it becomes clear that your assailant plans to kill you, we recommend the following tactics: (1) Talk. Say "I have terminal cancer, and I'll die within a few months anyway." William Proxmire, a United States Senator, did just that a few years ago and was released unharmed by two gun-wielding captors. (2) Offer the man money or jewelry. (3) Stall for time by asking for a final request, a cigarette, or time to pray. There is a dual purpose for stalling and talking to your assailant. First, he may change his mind and free you (but don't count on it). Second, as you are talking, you may be able to move within arm's reach of his gun. As you move slowly toward him, do not make any gestures with your hands; try to remain calm and just keep talking. Once you are very close, the technique to use is similar to the one we recommend when an assailant has a knife. If the gun is in the assassin's right hand, thrust your right arm diagonally across your body, grasp the gun barrel, and force it out and away from your body. Simultaneously, deliver a finger jab into his eyes. Immediately get behind the assailant, moving in the direction away from the gun in case it goes off. Then quietly hurry toward safety. (See Figure 5–8.)

Getting behind the assailant minimizes your chances of being shot if he fires blindly in front of him. Running as quietly as possible *without screaming* is recommended for the same purpose—namely, to decrease your chance of being shot by your blinded assailant.

Many gunshot wounds, despite the fact that they look fatal, bleed severely, or involve vital body areas, need not stop your counterattack. Therefore, no matter what you feel if shot, execute a thumb gouge to the eyes with whatever strength you have. As we recommended for the knife attack, once you have blinded your assailant and if he has dropped his weapon, do not pick it up. Quietly and quickly flee to safety. Never pick up the gun, and never attempt to shoot him with it.

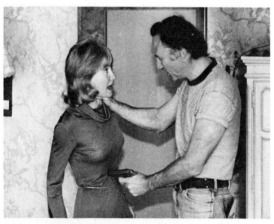

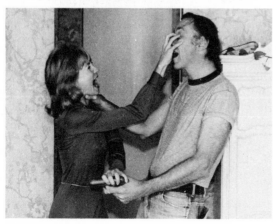

FIG. 5-8.
DEFENSE AGAINST
A GUN.

Bludgeon Attack

Various objects can be wielded by an assailant to strike a woman. Axes, lamps, vases, hammers, pipes, and sticks have been used to crush skulls. Never try to block such a blow. You would most likely be clobbered by your own arm as well as the bludgeon. Only a woman who is a martial-arts expert could successfully foil such a blow. Your best tactic is to scream and leap toward your assailant while reaching up with both hands to execute a thumb gouge. (See Figure 5–9.) By getting close to his body you will avoid receiving the momentum of his blow and be properly positioned to attack his eyes. Follow through by delivering kicks to the head before fleeing. Do not pick up his weapon, and do not use it on him.

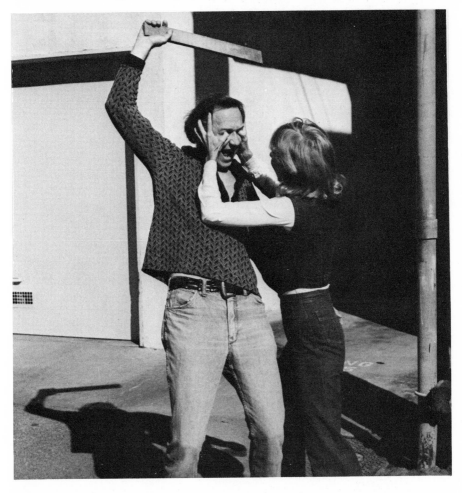

FIG. 5-9
DEFENSE AGAINST A BLUDGEON.

Summary

Our discussion stresses that you should not rely on physical weapons for fighting. Your voice, fingers and thumbs, knees, hands, and legs are the only weapons you need. The suggested weapons we described maybe helpful if easily accessible, but you must develop confidence in yourself rather than relying on such items. This advice also applies when you are defending yourself against attack from a bludgeon, a knife, or a gun. Your body and common sense are defensive weapons you cannot purchase in a store.

Chapter 6
Fourteen Dangerous Situations

If this book were thousands of pages long, we still could not cover all possible dangerous situations. To solve this problem, we have limited our discussion to fourteen commonly encountered dangers. As we review them, try to imagine how they could happen to you, where they could happen to you, and what tactics you would use if they did happen to you.

As we stressed in previous chapters, mental preparedness achieved by imagining yourself confronted with danger is a key to your overall strategy for personal protection. An excellent way to jog your imagination is to read newspaper stories and watch TV programs and movies about violence. Unfortunately they are not too hard to find. Empathize with the victims, and try to figure out ways you would have eliminated, avoided, or reacted to the dangers.

Bunco

Bunco crimes are those in which victims are lied to by charming thieves who seduce them into believing a story and induce them to part with their money. The proof that P. T. Barnum was correct when he said "A sucker is born every minute" is the very existence of bunco. Here are some examples of how these con artists work.

The phone of an unsuspecting victim rings. "Hello, I'm Mr. Jenoway, a federal inspector from your bank. The manager, Mr. Lewis—

you know him, don't you?—asked me to contact you about helping us in our investigation. He said you are a law-abiding citizen, and we need someone who is above suspicion in order to catch a crooked teller who is stealing cash." The con man then convinces his victim to meet him in front of the bank where he explains his or her role. The victim is to withdraw a large sum of cash, which the con artist states will immediately be marked by the FBI and returned to him or her. The victim will then put the money back in his or her account, not losing even a day's interest, so that the FBI can apprehend the teller with the marked money when he steals it. The only mark in this bunco scheme is our good samaritan victim. When the con artist pretends to go to the FBI and have the money marked, he never returns.

Another common bunco scheme works because of the victim's greed. A well-groomed con man stops a potential victim and shows him or her an envelope. In it is a pile of paper with a hundred dollar bill clearly visible on top. "I just found this envelope and if you'll help me find the owner I'll share the reward. I need your help because I'm leaving town for a week on business and can't carry all this cash with me. Why, there must be fifty thousand dollars stuffed in here." The con artist continues, "I'll let you hold all the money if you'll give me two thousand dollars as 'good faith' to prove your honesty. You'll get the two thousand dollars back when we receive the reward." He then escorts his victim to the bank where he or she withdraws the money. The exchange takes place, the con man gets $2,000 of the victim's money, and the victim gets an envelope containing only $100. A good deal for the bunco artist.

The deceptive repairman-bunco artist works like this. Dressed in a repairman's uniform, driving a labeled truck, and carrying false identification, he appears at your door to offer a "company special." If you give him your sewing machine and twenty-five dollars, the company will completely recondition and update it. One enterprising bunco expert we know of used this scheme to obtain over 200 sewing machines and $5,000 in cash, left town, and was never seen again.

Another type of consumer fraud is called the Gypsy Scam. In this operation a well-groomed door-to-door salesman offers cut-rate home improvements such as roofing or driveway resurfacing. "We can offer you a half-price deal because our crew is in your neighborhood, and we want to keep them busy between regular jobs." Cash is generally demanded upon completion of the job, which is done in a slipshod manner and with substandard materials. The workmen disappear after milking a neighborhood, thus earning their name of Gypsies. When the rain floods the living room and the driveway buckles, the Gypsies are busy offering bargains in other neighborhoods far away.

To prevent becoming the victim of a bunco artist is simple. Only conduct business with people whose reputation precedes them. Just as you choose a doctor by recommendation from friends, relatives, or a medical society, so you should do business with people who are recommended to you by friends, relatives, the Better Business Bureau, or Chamber of Commerce.

Recognizing and avoiding the bunco scheme is also simple. Any offer that sounds too good to be true is precisely that. When you learn of a businss deal from a stranger and you feel greed bubbling up inside, flash a red light. Here are ten golden rules for your protection:

1. Know that bunco artists and swindlers abound.
2. Know that anyone can be a target.
3. Know the people with whom you are dealing.
4. Know all the terms of a contract.
5. Know how much you can lose as well as gain.
6. Use only established, reputable businesses and agencies.
7. Use the services of reputable lawyers when large sums are involved.
8. Use legal financial channels for conducting business, such as your bank or stockbroker.
9. Use time and patience and avoid quick deals.
10. Use your common sense.

One final word. Unfortunately, many victims of bunco artists are so embarrassed by their stupidity at being swindled that they fail to contact the police. Bunco artists count on this to stay in business. Like rape, robbery, assault, and other major crimes, bunco is serious and should be reported to the police immediately. Even if you are only an intended victim and manage to elude the scheme, it is your obligation to report the attempt to the police.

Dating Dangers

How Not to Meet Men

Women from time immemorial have been beset with the problem of how to safely meet new and interesting men. A good way we know is to be "fixed up" by a mutual friend or relative. If possible, the first meeting or date should be with this friend, thus assuring safety and some degree of social compatibility. What we do not recommend is simply meeting a stranger in a bar, on the street, or while driving. In such situations danger is maximum. Between these extremes are social settings in which men and women come together because of a common interest. School activities, social clubs, church groups, and political organizations are good examples of such meeting places. Caution is still necessary because many potential assailants are clever enough to go to socially acceptable functions just to pick a victim for rape, robbery, or murder.

When discussing dating with young women, we advise them to take things "one step at a time." If a man is interested in forming a meaningful relationship with you, he will understand this. For example, if you meet a man while playing tennis with a friend and he invites you out for coffee or offers to drive you home, it is best to arrange another meeting in a public place. If he is seriously interested, he will agree to meet you later. Don't get into his car, don't give him your phone number or address, and don't accept an invitation to his home.

Four Commonsense Rules for Dating

Wear appropriate clothing. Whether you are fifteen or fifty, your clothes tell a story to anyone who looks at you.

Avoid provocative words and actions. Don't tease. Don't promise or suggest something that you do not intend to give. There is a thin line between being friendly, being flirtatious, and being sexually provocative. It should be easy to recognize when a date makes improper advances. Women, however, have reported to us that they were surprised or shocked by fellows getting "fresh" after half-hour necking sessions. We answer such women by noting with surprise that it took so long for their dates to get "fresh." Being able to recognize that a man is sexually aroused and sexually aggressive when on a date is as necessary as knowing how to drive if you are sitting behind the wheel of a car traveling sixty miles an hour. As in all potentially dangerous situations, early recognition and slowing down immediately are best.

Don't go where you know you won't be comfortable. This means avoiding situations where you know there will be people indulging in activities in which you do not want to participate. For example, if you know that your friends are going to a party where drugs, alcohol, or sexual promiscuity will take place, don't go along.

Avoid driving to isolated areas. Parking in lovers' lanes and stopping "just to watch the stars" may be dangerous, even if your date is a perfect gentleman. Dangers lurk outside in such secluded rendezvous. Avoiding these places may cause you to lose a date, but if he is dating you for the purpose of taking you to such places, it is better to eliminate him from your list.

How to Handle an Overzealous Date

If your date becomes overzealous, talking is your first and best means of discouraging his sexual advances. The simple and direct approach is wisest. "No, I don't want to do that." Avoid arguments and statements such as "I don't know you well enough" or "I'm not that kind of girl." "No" is "No," and you are entitled to your conviction. If your date is a gentleman and is sensitive to your wishes, he will stop. If he does not stop, you must either go to a public area where he cannot continue to annoy you or leave him. There are many tactful ways to accomplish both of these. For example, you may suggest that you return to "the party" if he has taken you to a secluded area, or you can say you must go to the toilet. Telling a man that you are having menstrual cramps, that you feel sick to your stomach and may vomit, or that you have epilepsy and must go home for your medication are all ploys that have been used successfully.

Certain psychological disturbances could prompt men to press their advances beyond the point at which reason or a simulated illness works. Under such rare circumstances your "date" then becomes a "serious assailant," and a full-fledged counterattack to immobilize him may be necessary.

Vicious Dog

It is surprising to many students to learn that each year hundreds of women are scared and maimed by dogs. Even friendly appearing or familiar dogs can suddenly turn vicious and attack without warning. Thus some knowledge of dog behavior is necessary if you are to be prepared to defend yourself. While we would never purport to be dog psychologists, here are a few generalizations about how a dog reacts.

Unless it is trained to attack, a dog will fight a person only under most unusual circumstances. For example, dogs will attack when personally threatened, when their owner or puppies are threatened, when they are sick or in pain, or when they are starving. Your best strategy when faced by an angry dog is to allay its fears of any possible threat you might present. The more you can calm a dog, the less likely it is to attack.

Like people, dogs prepare themselves for attack and thus give warning. Crouching, barking, and snarling are signals of impending attack. If you heed these warnings and back away, a dog may calm down. Never ignore such preattack behaviors.

Showing fear may increase your chances of being attacked. A dog can sense human emotion; if you are frightened, it may become more alarmed. It will crouch and snarl, further frightening you. If you raise your hand in fear, the dog may take this as a threat of an impending blow and lunge. This vicious cycle has led to many innocent victims needing sutures and to many dogs being labeled vicious and destroyed. The lesson in all this is as follows: (1) Do not show fear to a dog. (2) Do not jump at or run away from a dog. (3) Do not scream at a dog. Instead, talk to the dog in a calm, firm voice, then walk quickly and quietly away.

Let us assume the worst! A dog's attack is successful, and it sinks its teeth into your arm. Don't pull away, because that will tear your skin. Rather, jab into the dog's eyes or kick it in the groin. If you are bitten, it is crucial to find out if the dog has had antirabies shots. Thus you must obtain a complete description for the police. Every dog bite should be treated by a physician. There are dangers other than rabies, and dog bites usually require special cleaning.

Gang of Small Children

Although it's difficult to believe, even "nice" children can at times be very menacing and dangerous. The primary reason is that kids are susceptible to group suggestions and pressures, and when goaded on by their friends, some kids will do anything to "prove themselves." When you are walking alone, you are a perfect target for group taunts and attacks.

If you are confronted by a hostile group of kids, your strategy, as always, should be to avoid trouble. Try to ignore them and walk quickly to safety. Never argue or respond to taunts. If you cannot flee to safety, cast intimidating looks at all of them, which will most likely frighten the children and make them disperse. If they do not and you must physically defend yourself, kick at their knees. If they continue and your health is threatened, execute groin pulls and eye gouges. Although they may be young, if their intent is to injure you you must have no qualms about injuring them in order to get away.

Woman Beating

The men who beat women suffer from a neurotic illness. They are driven by unconscious needs to act out emotions and scenes from their repressed childhood. They are as unable to consciously control their behavior to stop beating as compulsive alcoholics are unable to give up drinking. Between bouts of beating, they suffer guilt, remorse, shame, and all the emotions that, in normal people, would lead to a change in behavior. But these emotions in women beaters do not vaccinate them, nor do they protect their victims from the next attack. This illness does not respect or favor a particular race, creed, color, shape, size, social class, or occupation. The most unlikely of men as judged by such general characteristics as gentleness, courteousness, and deference to women can be women beaters. In fact, we know of several cases in which the man exaggerated his deferential attitudes toward women both out of guilt and to support his denial. "You've seen how I respect my wife, doctor, and how courteous I always am. I might have shoved her when she pushed me, but I'd never start anything. I'd certainly never beat her up." This type of denial is actually a confession, and it indicates no insight and no chance of cure. Indeed, without an acknowledgment of the problem, personal effort, and the help of professionals, the prognosis for the illness called woman beating is bleak.

The victims of habitual woman beaters are of three types. First, there are those who are beaten once or twice, recognize the seriousness and extent of their situations, and terminate their relationships with the men who beat them.

The second type of victims have a neurotic illness that fits hand in glove with their beaters' illnesses. Like them, they are unconsciously driven to act out emotions and scenes from their repressed childhoods. In their cases they have identified with the victims in their pasts. They are so in need of this unconscious gratification, despite protest to the contrary and the actual physical suffering they receive, that they keep coming back for more. The proof of this lies in the fact that they stay in relationships in which they are repeatedly brutalized, even disfigured, and in some cases, maimed. Yet, they refuse to "blow the whistle" on their "loved ones." Emergency-room physicians are familiar with these repeated "victims." While wincing in pain, while the black-and-blue bruises are swelling, or while their bones are being set, they curse their "loved ones" and vow to leave them. "Never again," they say. Unfortunately, by the time they return for a checkup, wounds healed, they are exuding excuses and heaping blame on themselves. "If I'd just kept the kids quiet and had dinner ready like I promised, I wouldn't have made him mad." "Look, Doc, I know how mean he gets when he's drunk, and I knew he was drunk, so I should have stayed out of his way." Such women often resurrect chauvinistic attitudes from the past to rationalize their subjugation and beatings. Even in the 1980s we hear such ridiculous rationalizations as "He's my husband and he has a right to beat me." Or worse, we're all familiar with the sad saying "I know he loves me because he still beats me."

The third type of victim is the woman who is in the process of terminating her relationship with a woman beater who will not let her go. Just like two clasped hands, both must relax for the grip to be broken, but many men refuse to let go. They blackmail, cajole, threaten, and follow their victims. The only refuges available to such unfortunate women are shelters for battered women, the police, and if their life or health is at stake, fighting.

Our recommendations to a woman who is involved with a habitual beater are simple. First, leave him immediately. Accept no excuses or rationalizations. Turn a deaf ear. If you are too emotionally entangled with a woman beater to leave him, admit that you need professional help and get it. The department of psychiatry or clinical psychology at a nearby university, your county medical association, and your local government-sponsored mental health clinic are excellent sources for referrals. The time and effort spent on such treatment could prove lifesaving. One woman in treatment used this rationalization for staying with her husband: "Even though he beats me up, he's a good father to our three children, and children need a father at home." Through treatment, she was able to accept the fact that her husband was setting a dangerous example for their children. They were already demonstrating delinquent behavior by becoming the bullies of their neighborhood and beating up young children. She also uncovered painful memories from her own childhood of watching in panic her drunken father's rages. Although he never hit her mother, she identified with her mother's terror and came unconsciously to need this in her marital relationship. When freed from these unconscious shackles, she was able to terminate her marriage because her husband refused to join her in treatment.

Until now our recommendations have been based on the first two strategies of the Conroy Method of Self-defense: Eliminate, recognize, and avoid danger. There may, however, come a time when a woman's very life is at stake at the hands of a woman beater. If this is the case, fighting back may be necessary. By fighting back we mean attacking with such ferocity that you incapacitate the attacker in order to flee to safety. This is psychologically difficult enough against an unknown assailant. It is doubly difficult when the person is someone with whom you have had a long-term relationship. Therefore, we caution you, don't fight unless you intend to incapacitate.

To illustrate this point, we wish to relate the following true story. During the eighth week of a ten-week class at California State University, a student startled us when she arrived in class with a black eye, a swollen lip, and visible cuts on her arms and legs. We asked her what happened, and she began a bitter tirade against the Conroy Method of Self-defense. The gist of her story was that she attempted to stop her husband from going drinking with his pals. They argued to the point at which he pushed her into a chair. She sprang up, blocked the door with her body, snatched the car keys from his hand, dropped them down her blouse, and threatened "I know self-defense and if you touch me, I'll use it on you." The result was predictable. He grabbed for the keys, she timidly kicked his shin, and he became enraged. He slapped her across the face and shoved her so forcibly away from the door that she flew over the couch and crashed through the glass top of the coffee table. He stormed out without so much as a word or even a glance back at his injured wife.

The remainder of the class was spent discussing what had happened to this poor woman. The consensus was as follows: First, rather than eliminating danger her threats had created it. Second, by failing to recognize and avoid danger, she further angered her husband by taking his keys and blocking his way. Third, fighting was uncalled for since neither her life nor health was in danger. Furthermore, once having made the decision to attack, she fought incorrectly. She failed to follow our dictum that the only purpose of fighting is to incapacitate and flee. She should not have fought unless she was willing to yank his testicles, break his knee, or blind him. By the end of the class, the victim agreed that she had erred. Everyone supported the recommendation that she and her husband seek professional counseling.

Once again, the prognosis for habitual women beaters is grim. Unfortunately, clinical evidence indicates that more often these men change their victims rather than their ways.

Violent Women

Because of a host of sociological factors, the role of women has changed markedly over the past several years. The vast majority of these changes have been beneficial to women and represent victories against repressive stereotypes. An alarming side effect, however, has occurred. It involves a small number of women who have chosen to emulate men in the use of violence. These women have severe psychological problems that are expressed by physically assaulting others. Thus we have to caution you to be prepared to defend yourself from assaults by other women. Police statistics show conclusively that the number of violent crimes by women is on the upsurge. Teenage gangs of girls are increasing in schools because "being tough" is a badge of courage for their members. Further evidence of this trend is sadly supplied by the fact that fringe or extremist political groups have many female terrorists in their ranks. Therefore your thinking about general principles of personal safety must be extended to include women as well as men. "Her" must be substituted for "him" when assessing possible dangers.

Your methods of attack are slightly modified when danger exists from a woman. As before, we advise you to fight only when your life is in danger and there is no means of escape. The vulnerable areas on a woman are the same as those on a man with the exception of the groin. Blows directed to a woman's groin will hurt rather than seriously injure her. Initiate your attack with a scream, attack the most easily accessible vulnerable areas, and follow through until the woman is immobilized. Many students believe that to strike a woman in the breast or to pull her hair would be particularly painful and render a female assailant helpless. These are misconceptions. Since the purpose of your attack is to incapacitate your assailant, aim for her eyes, neck, and knees. (See Figure 6–1.)

FIG. 6-1
DEFENSE AGAINST
A WOMAN.

Burglary

Burglary is defined as "breaking and entering with the intent to commit a felony." The FBI estimates that there are approximately 3.5 million burglaries committed each year. Over three-quarters of all burglaries involve forcible entry, with 19 percent unlawful entries (without force) and the remaining 8 percent forcible entry attempts.

The vast majority of burglars, unlike murderers, get away with their crime. Recent FBI estimates are that only 16 percent of burglaries are solved. As with robbery, most arrested burglars are young: 84 percent are under twenty-one years of age with 51 percent being under the age of eighteen.

Should you be the victim of a burglary, be sure to report it immediately. Burglars frequently operate in one neighborhood or according to a specific modus operandi. Your information, pieced together with other reports, can help the police trap the burglar.

Some burglars are very clever and use their unwitting victims to learn when to strike. Here are some true cases from police files.

Mrs. Pine answers her phone.

Caller: "Good evening, Mrs. Pine. I'm conducting a survey for the research-development department at CBS television. The purpose of this study is to determine a profile of our viewers and their preferences. May I ask you a few questions regarding your viewing habits?"

Mrs. Pine: "Yes." (delighted to express her ideas for CBS)

Caller: "Approximately how much television do you watch during the day?"

Mrs. Pine: "Well, since I work until five, I don't watch TV until I get home, just before the six o'clock news."

Caller: "Does anyone in your household watch TV during the day?"

Mrs. Pine: "No, my husband works and the kids are in school until four. (Mrs. Pine just unwittingly informed her caller that her house is empty all day—a perfect invitation for a burglar.)

Caller: "How often do you watch television in the evenings?"

Mrs. Pine: "Well, Friday night seems to be the only time I can actually sit down and watch all evening because the kids are away playing church basketball and my husband is the coach." (Mrs. Pine just revealed that on Friday night she is home alone—a perfect invitation for a rapist.)

Caller: "Now, Mrs. Pine, in order to develop a profile of a one-night-a-week viewer, I'd like to ask you some personal questions. This information will be kept strictly confidential." (At this point the prospective rapist elicits information regarding Mrs. Pine's age, race, height, weight, and family income. He confirms her address from the phone book and thanks her. On the following Friday he put his ill-gotten information to use.)

Mrs. Wagner, newly divorced, was anxious to sell her furniture and move into her sister's condominium. She placed a "for sale"notice in her church bulletin. A woman phoned, pretending to be a fellow church member. Mrs. Wagner described the furniture, its cost, and was delighted when the caller indicated it was just what she was looking for. The caller asked if she could drop over Wednesday afternoon. When Mrs. Wagner agreed, the caller apologetically said she had just remembered a previous engagement for Wednesday, but could she make it Friday? "No," Mrs. Wagner replied. "I have my bridge club at one o'clock, and I won't be back until after four." "Could someone else in the house show me the furniture?" asked the caller. "I'm sorry, but no one will be home." The two women then agreed to meet on Saturday, and Mrs. Wagner gave directions to her apartment. On Friday afternoon the burglar's accomplices followed the directions and emptied the apartment. A neighbor said she saw men putting furniture into a van, but she thought nothing of it because she knew Mrs. Wagner was moving.

Janet Rodrigues decided to sell her late-model Fiat. She placed an ad in the *Los Angeles Times*. Among the people who called was a man asking specific questions about the condition of the car's battery, muffler, tires, and stereo tape deck. When she assured him they were all in perfect condition, he asked to see the car. Mrs. Rodrigues agreed to meet him the following morning in her carport and gave him her address. The next morning she discovered he had come early and left with her battery, tires, stereo tape deck, and hub caps.

Terry Millar, having quarreled with her boyfriend, was delighted to go away on a ski weekend with friends. "I'll show him I'm not sitting around waiting for the phone to ring." Angrily she left the following recording on her answering machine: "Hi, this is Terry. I've gone to Lake Tahoe for the weekend and won't be back until Sunday. Please leave your name and number, and I'll return your call Sunday night." Her burglars appreciated her recording so much that they stole the answering machine along with everything else in her apartment.

Mr. Marques, a professional burglar, scanned the morning paper to plan his work for the day. There, on the third page, was his first job. A picture of Mr. and Mrs. Brooks, winners of a two-week vacation in Hawaii. Even the itinerary was listed, including a 7:30 A.M. departure that day on United Airlines. He found his second job in the obituary section. At 11:30 A.M. there would be a funeral for Dr. Lennard R. Rutherford III, at the Chapel of the Flowers mortuary. Mr. Rutherford was reported to be a famous gun and art collector. Since everyone who knew him would probably attend the funeral, his house would be an easy mark. An eleven o'clock phone call confirmed this. And finally, his third job, Miss Lisa Bauman was marrying Mr. Bob Steinberg at 4:30 today at the Biltmore Hotel, where a reception would follow. Miss Bauman, the article stated, is the daughter of Dr. and Mrs. Cliesh Bauman of Pacific Palisades. The burglar simply checked his phone book for the Baumans' address and collected Lisa's wedding gifts to conclude a profitable day.

Mrs. Hu, owner of a well-known, rare jade collection, received a phone call shortly after her husband left for work. The caller stated that he was a doctor at the Saint Benedict Hospital. He said that Mr. Hu had been in a tragic car accident, was in critical condition, and she must come to the hospital immediately! When she reached the hospital, she discovered that her husband was not there. When she returned home, her jade collection was not there either.

In conclusion, common sense should tell you that anyone, including burglars and rapists, can read your advertisements and announcements in public media. Careful wording is therefore necessary to assure your safety. Your common sense should also tell you to never divulge personal information to anyone you do not know and trust.

Forceful Intruder

Imagine you have failed to use proper precautions, such as a through-the-door peephole, and that a man is standing in your doorway. You sense that your caller is not who he represents himself to be. You try to close the door but can't because he is forcing it open. Your strategy is to get the door closed and call the police. Since he is using force on the door, you must assume that he will use force on you if he gets in. Your best tactic is instantaneous attack. Scream and allow the door to open just enough to execute a finger jab to his eyes. As he clutches his eyes in pain, slam the door. Immediately lock and bolt the door and all other possible means of entry. Then call the police. (See Figure 6–2.)

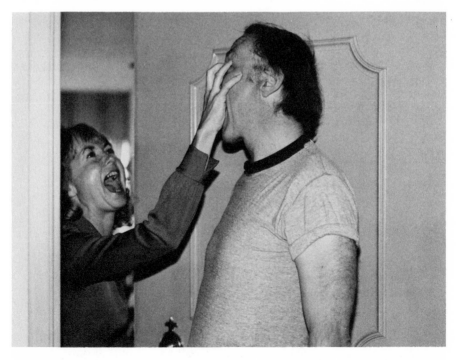

FIG. 6-2
DEFENSE AGAINST A FORCEFUL INTRUDER.

Threat of Being Bound by an Assailant

We are often asked during lectures how a person should react if an assailant threatens to tie him or her up. This seemingly simple question has no simple answer. Your emotional makeup and your evaluation of the situation determine the answer. For our part, allowing oneself to be tied should be avoided if at all possible because it precludes fighting and fleeing to safety. There are, of course, situations in which you must comply, such as when confronted by multiple assailants with weapons.

An assailant will bind his victim for one of three reasons. One, to aid his escape; two, to torture; or three, to kill. If his motive is to aid his escape, talking your way out of being tied may be possible. By following our strategy of complying with a robber, you will have given him valuables, demonstrated cooperation, and assured him that you pose no threat. Tell him that you will not pursue him, that you won't report the robbery (lying is justified in this circumstance), and even volunteer to be locked in a closet to aid his escape. If, at this point, an assailant still insists on binding you, assume that his motive is other than to escape and be alert for the next opportunity to fight. Pretending to cooperate while about to be bound should provide you with the opportunity to attack, incapacitate him, and flee.

Our philosophy regarding not being bound is based on many news accounts of sadistic murders committed on helplessly bound victims. In our own neighborhood, a recent robbery ended in murder. Four employees of a Torrance, California, movie theater opened a safe, submitted to being bound, and then were brutally slaughtered by having their throats slashed "ear to ear." The well-known contemporary author Truman Capote chronicled a similar tragedy. In his book *In Cold Blood*, he described the deaths of a family bound by murderers who assured them that they were being tied up to abet the assailants' escape. This true story points out how irrational and unpredictable murderers are. Capote related how the murderers, when interrogated, confessed that they first bound their victims to aid their escape. Then, realizing that "dead men tell no tales," they decided to "guarantee their escape" by slaying the witnesses.

Robbery

Robbery is defined by the FBI Uniform Crime Report as "the taking or attempting to take anything of value from the care, custody, or control of a person or persons by force or threat of force or violence and/or by putting the victim in fear." About one-half million robberies occur in the United States per year. This is just under one-half of all the crimes of violence reported in the country. These figures prove that most assaults on individuals are committed by robbers who are intent on stealing something.

The chances of your being robbed are greater if you live in a large city than in a rural area. Nearly one-half of all robberies are committed in the streets by men under twenty-one years of age. Astoundingly enough, approximately one-third of all robbers are under the age of eighteen. Guns are most often used (42 percent), the threat of force (33 percent), knives (13 percent), and other weapons (12 percent).

The following headline appeared in our local newspaper last month: HIGH SCHOOL HONOR STUDENT STABBED TO DEATH WHILE DEFENDING HER MOTHER FROM PURSE SNATCHERS. This horrible tragedy could easily have been prevented if this girl had studied self-defense. She would not have leaped into the air, kicking the assailant in the throat and smashing him to the concrete. No, that's for TV and the movies. The Conroy Method of Self-defense would have taught her to relinquish her mother's purse quickly. (See Figure 6–3.)

A bizarre tragedy recently occurred in San Francisco. An elderly couple was walking their dog when they were approached by a neighborhood child. "Give me your money!" demanded the young boy. The irascible old man shoved him aside and told him to "get lost." The youngster brandished a handgun and with no further conversation shot the man in the chest, killing him. As unlikely as this incident may seem, it and other similar tragedies do occur.

Your tactics when you are confronted by a robber, whether at home or elsewhere, are simple. Listen carefully so that you are sure of what he wants. If it is something specific like your wallet, simply give it to him quickly. Do not engage in conversation. If you are at home, and he wants certain valuables, tell him where they are. Anything in your home, except your health, can be repurchased. After getting what he wants, a professional robber will be as eager to get away as you are to have him go.

It is important to obtain a clear description of the thief to aid the police in apprehending him. (See Chapter 9.) If he gives you instructions such as "Don't call the police," agree with him no matter how ridiculous it sounds. Once you are certain he has gone, immediately contact the police. You must report every incident, even if the theft is small. This is not merely your responsibility as a good citizen; if his career continues unabated, he may harm others and even return to you.

Special mention must be made of the drug-addicted robber who is in desperate need of money to support his habit. He may say irrational things or act in a bizarre way if he is having withdrawal symptoms. Meeting his demands quickly is particularly essential. If he thinks you are trying to stall, he may become incensed and will be more likely to attack.

During a recent outbreak of purse snatchings in the Los Angeles area, many women began carrying their purses in paper sacks. One bag snatcher was in for a big surprise. According to the *Los Angeles Times*, Hollis Sharp, age fifty, walked her dog every evening and carried a paper bag and shovel to clean up after him. One night having collected a particularly large amount of refuse, Ms. Sharp was accosted by a six-foot 175-pound robber. He grabbed her from behind and snatched her brown bag. Imagine the look on his face when he reached in the bag to retrieve his stolen goods. (Nice going, Ms. Sharp!)

FIG. 6-3
DEFENSE AGAINST A ROBBER—GIVE HIM YOUR VALUABLES.

Two or More Assailants

We must begin this section with a word about group psychology. Even the "nicest" group of teenage boys or young men can be dangerous. For example, they may approach you in an isolated setting; and while not having planned a robbery or an attack, they may get the idea that here is a chance for some "innocent fun." "Hey, Charlie, she looks like your type," says one. "Yeah, Charlie, you said you are a great lover," says another. A few more remarks like this, and Charlie, light-headed from a few beers, decides to prove his masculinity. "Come on, fellows, I'll show you how it's done." Before you know it, you are surrounded. Your strategy is to get away without a physical confrontation. Therefore, your first tactic is to talk, but don't talk to Charlie. Do not respond to his lewd remarks and, most important, try to remain calm. Looking confidently at another member of the group, say "Look, fellows, I don't want any trouble" and walk slowly toward safety. In this way you may diffuse a volatile and potentially violent situation. If the men continue to tease and insult you, keep walking. Remember, "Words can never hurt you."

Another type of danger occurs when two or more assailants have singled you out for robbery or rape. With such men talking will give you time to discover what they want. If they ask for money or valuables, quickly comply with their request. If they want to rape you, attempt to talk them out of it. (See Chapter 8 for suggestions.) If three or more men attempt to rape you and you believe they'll let you go without serious physical injury, you may decide to submit. Fighting off one assailant may be difficult. Fighting three assailants is three times as difficult.

If the assailants intend to kill you and it becomes necessary to fight in order to save your life, how do you attack two or three men? As in other situations, your attack consists of screams, eye gouges, groin pulls, hand blows, and kicks. In this situation, initiate your attack on the closest man. However, when one member of a group starts an attack, respond as if they all attacked. Each and every one is a fair target for your blows. (See Figure 6–4.)

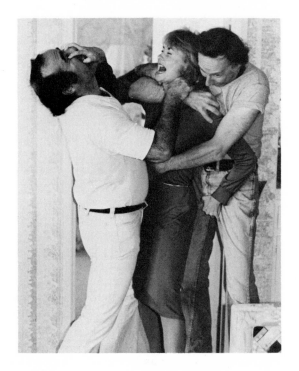

FIG. 6-4
DEFENSE AGAINST
TWO ASSAILANTS.

Aggravated Assault

The FBI Uniform Crime Report defines aggravated assault as "an unlawful attack by one person upon another for the purpose of inflicting severe or aggravated bodily injury." This crime constitutes slightly more than half of all reported crimes of violence. Most assaults occur during the summer, and approximately one-fourth of the aggravated assaults are committed with a gun. Knives account for 23 percent, blunt objects for 27 percent, and personal weapons such as hands and feet for 25 percent. As with robbery, persons under twenty-one years of age accounted for 31 percent of those arrested for aggravated assault.

If you are a victim of an aggravated assault, you will probably want to fight immediately. No matter what disadvantage you may have initially, whether you are hit, kicked, or stabbed, fight 100 percent.

Murder

The FBI Uniform Crime Report defines murder and nonnegligent manslaughter as "the willful killing of one human being by another." Most murders occur in the month of December, are committed with guns, and the victims are usually men between the ages of twenty and twenty-four.

Approximately 20,000 murders occur each year in the United States, and they account for 2 to 3 percent of all violent crimes. Cutting and stabbing instruments account for 19 percent, while guns are the most frequently used weapons (63 percent). In a November 22, 1980, *Los Angeles Times* article, Phil Kerby drew a startling comparison. "The nation was shocked by its losses in Vietnam," he wrote. "During the peak seven years of the war, more than 40,000 American soldiers died in action. Yet in that same period, more than 50,000 American civilians were murdered with handguns." He continued, "The Massachusetts Institute of Technology did a crime study for the National Science Foundation and the results were profoundly disturbing. The survey found, for example, that a child born in 1974 in the nation's capital has one chance in 36 of being murdered during his lifetime, and the risk is even greater in several other large metropolitan areas."

An often-quoted and accurate statistic is that murderers know their victims. In fact, according to a recent FBI Uniform Crime Report, 20 percent of the victims were killed by their immediate family. Another 40 percent were killed by acquaintances, including boyfriends, girl friends, and neighbors; and only 13 percent by strangers.

Consider the frightening fact that 25 percent of the murder victims are killed during the course of a robbery. This indicates to us that many victims might be alive today had they followed the Conroy Method of Self-defense. Our basic instructions to cooperate with robbers undoubtedly could have saved lives. Many murderers have told police that they were "forced" to kill by resisting victims when all they wanted was "to take something and run."

The chances of a murderer getting away with his crime are less than those for any major crime. In fact, about three-quarters of all murders are solved.

Any of the dangerous situations described in this chapter could result in a battle for your life. At the moment you realize the possibility of your death, you are most likely to panic. Your panic and fear must be converted to rage. A person who tries to kill you deserves your full wrath. Any hesitancy you may have about blinding, paralyzing, or even killing someone should be ignored. Both moral and religious laws recognize homicide as justified when committed in self-defense. An attack upon your life demands your ultimate counterattack. Keep in mind that many victims, when realizing that they are about to be murdered, possess enormous strength and energy.

Your tactics for attack are those described previously and carried out to their extreme. Kicks, gouges, jabs, and blows must be repeated. Concentrate on the most vulnerable areas such as the eyes and the groin. Continue your attack until you are absolutely certain that the murderer is immobilized or unconscious.

Rape-Murder

In this section we shall discuss rape-murder, the most horrible and frightening crime of all. It is the terror of which nightmares are made. By studying the material in this chapter you will decrease the chance of becoming a victim of this rare crime. Try to overcome the natural repugnance and rationalization of thinking "Rape-murder is so rare that I don't need to be concerned with it."

It is a sad fact that when a mass rape-murderer is at large, self-defense classes are overflowing, but when the headlines cease, the demand subsides. The explanation for this was offered in Chapter 1, when we discussed the psychological mechanism called denial. We reported how thoughts that are uncomfortable and produce anxiety are actively pushed from our conscious mind and denied or forgotten. Thus, when there is no rape-murderer in the headlines, it is easy for you to deny the possibility that this most horrible of crimes happens, and as a result, you lower your preparedness.

The horrifying and repulsive cases described in this section are based on actual histories of five rape-murderers. As you form a mental image of their personalities, how they selected and stalked their victims, and how they sexually assaulted and killed them, think to yourself: "How could I have eliminated being selected?" or, if confronted, "What could I have done to recognize and avoid the danger?" Following the brief biography of each rape-murderer think of ways in which the victims could have eliminated or recognized and avoided the tragedies. We hope that the suggestions we present will serve as springboards for thoughts and for discussions.

W. M., twenty-nine years old, Caucasian,
male, business-machine operator,
four rape-murders

The anonymity and isolation of city living were glaringly brought to public attention in March 1964. Headlines blared out THIRTY-EIGHT WITNESS MURDER—NOT ONE HELPED. Throughout the country people were asking "How could this have occurred?" and "Why didn't someone get involved?" "Why didn't someone just call the police?" and "Would anyone help me if it happened to me?"

What led to these headlines and questions were these grisly facts. Kitty Genovese, a young single woman was walking alone to her apartment building in New York City at 3 A.M. Cruising the neighborhood in his white sports car that night in search of a victim was Winston Moseley. He was stalking a victim to add to his list of four rape-murders and five rapes. During his confession Moseley said, "I just set out to find any girl that was unattended and I was going to kill her. . . I could run much faster than she could. I jumped on her back and stabbed her several times." Kitty Genovese screamed, "Oh my God, I've been stabbed! Please help me." These first screams attracted the attention of a man in a neighboring apartment house who saw the assault. He yelled out of the window, "Let that girl alone." He did not bother to call the police or come to her assistance. When Moseley ran back to his car, Ms. Genovese struggled to her apartment lobby where she collapsed. In his confession Moseley stated: "I had a feeling this man would close his window and go back to sleep." His hunch was correct, and he pursued her after a few minutes when everything remained quiet. "She was twisting and turning, and I don't know how many times or where I stabbed her, until she was fairly quiet," Moseley continued. After she was unconscious, he tore off her clothes and raped her. During the final stabbings and rape, he told the court, "I heard the upstairs door open twice, maybe three times, but when I looked up there was nobody."

Review the facts of this crime while asking yourself what you could have done differently to: 1. Eliminate danger. For example, I could have (a) returned home early in the evening. (b) returned home with friends. (c) taken a cab and asked the driver to wait until I was safely in the apartment. (d) been accompanied by a large dog. 2. Recognize and avoid danger (once aware that I am being stalked). I could have (a) spotted Moseley's car cruising and parking nearby. (b) walked or run assertively. (c) screamed "fire, fire." (d) dropped my purse in hopes he would settle for money. 3. Fight. Speculate about what tactics you might use to be

most effective, once attacked. Keep in mind that Moseley's only weapon
was a knife and his first four stab wounds were not fatal.

A. D., thirty-one years old, Caucasian,
male, auto mechanic,
eleven rape-murders

For two years—between 1962 and 1964—women in the city of Boston were in the grip of fear. A man who was dubbed "The Boston Strangler" was rape-murdering at will, and the authorities were helpless to apprehend him. His victims were of all ages, including a seventy-five-and an eighty-five-year-old woman. He raped both black and white women, selecting them at random. "Attractiveness has nothing to do with it
. . . She was a woman," he is quoted as saying. When the "Boston Strangler" was finally apprehended, he was identified as Albert De Salvo, a former army prizefighter with a history of several assaults. He personally claimed that he had committed over 2,000 rapes. He confessed to identifying single women who lived alone by looking at apartment house directories. He was adept at posing as a repairman and used other lies to gain easy entry into dwellings. He said that if a perspective victim hesitated to let him in or challenged his veracity he would simply go somewhere else. If a victim fought back he would flee. De Salvo confessed that one large woman whom he attacked bit his finger to the bone. He was terrified and ran. De Salvo was reported to be neatly groomed, well-spoken, and charming. He was married and the father of two children.

De Salvo confessed that once he was alone with his victims in their apartment, he waited until their backs were turned and then grabbed them in a hammerlock. His modus operandi included disrobing his victims, tying stockings around their necks, biting and stabbing their breasts, placing their bodies in bizarre postures, sticking broomsticks and wine bottles into their vaginas, and performing sodomy on their dead bodies.

At this point, stop and imagine how you could have (1) eliminated being selected by De Salvo, (2) recognized and avoided being attacked, (3) fought him successfully. A few obvious answers are: (1) To eliminate danger don't identify yourself as a single woman on your apartment house register or in the phone book. (2) To recognize and avoid danger, don't allow strangers to talk their way into your house. Be certain that they have proper identification and verify it with their employer. (3) Fighting. How many of De Salvo's victims would be alive today if they had fought? No one can guess, but by De Salvo's own admission he fled when bitten by one victim whose courage kept her from becoming another murder statistic.

E. K., twenty-four years old, Caucasian,
male, unemployed,
six rape-murders

Next time you think that hitchhiking is a good means of transportation, consider the six young women who were picked up for the final ride of their lives by Edmund Emil Kemper III. While they were only concerned about reaching their destination, he was fantasizing, he confessed, of "killing women, cutting their heads off and eating them."

This "good samaritan" had the following personal history: He had dismembered and disfigured dolls and butchered his favorite cat at age nine while "praying with all my might that God would make everyone in the world die except me." He celebrated his fifteenth birthday by murdering his grandparents. His I.Q. of 136 allowed him to remember fantasies of killing and decapitating women from age nine on. It also aided in fooling authorities into releasing him from a prison for the criminally insane to which he had been committed. He celebrated his release from prison by murdering his mother and a neighbor. When he was twenty years old, six feet nine inches tall and weighing 280 pounds, he escaped detection over a six-month period while luring six women hitchhikers into his car, killing them, cutting them into pieces, and scattering their remains over the countryside. He even confessed to perverse sex acts with parts of dismembered bodies. Next time you're considering hitchhiking, remember this "good samaritan" who was so "accommodating to hitchhiking women."

We are certain that as you read this account you can think of many ways you could have avoided becoming one of Kemper's victims. We stress this fact: Never get into a stranger's car. We know of no circumstances that justify hitchhiking. Even if your car breaks down, stranding you in a desolate area and a well-meaning passerby offers you a ride, don't accept. Request that help be sent to you.

When you discuss fighting, consider Kemper's size. We have had students who thought it would be impossible to fight against a six-foot nine-inch giant weighing 280 pounds. But aren't his eyes just as vulnerable as a man four feet nine inches tall and weighing eighty pounds? Aren't his testicles just as tender? Yes!

K. B., twenty-seven years old, Caucasian, male, "psychologist," ten rape-murders

Act 1, scene 1: Location, glamorous Hollywood, California, discotheque. Characters: You and a girl friend, out for a night on the town; male lead, tall, slender, curly haired, ruggedly handsome with well-trimmed mustache, well-spoken, "clinical psychologist."

Act 1, scene 2: Male lead approaches you. He is complimentary and creates a favorable first impression.

Act 1, scene 3: After a delightful evening of dancing and mature conversation, male lead graciously offers you and your friend a ride home. Friend declines with a knowing wink to leave you a clear field.

Act 2, scene 1: Location, car interior on Hollywood Boulevard. Characters: You and "prince charming" are chatting as he drives past your turnoff and then begins to head toward Pasadena.

Act 2, scene 2: "A little ride" ends on hill overlooking the Rose Bowl.

Act 3, scene 1: Closeup of man's face as he attempts to strangle you to death. Dissolve, fade with montage of clothing being ripped, exposed body parts to indicate rape in progress.

In reality the "psychologist" was a part-time pimp, part-time security guard named Kenneth Bianchi, alias the "Hillside Strangler." Abandoned at two months of age and placed in foster homes until he was adopted at eleven months, he showed obvious emotional disturbances throughout his early years. At age eleven, he learned that he was adopted and was told that his real mother had been a "promiscuous barmaid." His adopted father died when Bianchi was fourteen, and his overbearing mother forced him to wear the dead man's shoes to the funeral. Following an abortive attempt at college and marriage, he turned to the streets to earn his living. Some of his victims were prostitutes, some were young runaways looking for a handout, while others were innocent victims he randomly selected or picked up socially with his cousin and accomplice Angelo Buono. Their smooth lines and good looks made meeting women easy. Moral of story: Good looks and good conversation should not lull you into forgetting that a stranger is a stranger. There is no substitute for getting to know someone over a period of time before trusting him. We hope these remarks serve as a springboard for thought and discussion. To increase your mental preparedness, decide how you would behave if placed in a similar situation.

R. S., twenty-two years old, Caucasian,
male, drifter, eight murders

Imagine an itinerant reaching a strange city and spending his last few dollars for heroin. Hopped up and broke, he decides to burglarize empty apartments to finance his next fix. Knocking on doors until he finds an unanswered open one, he enters and there to his surprise are nine sleeping young women. When they awake he brandishes a knife and demands their money. One of the women spits in his face and threatens to pick him out of a lineup. This infuriates him, and he single-handedly ties them up and drags them, one at a time, into another room. One brave woman suggests to the others that they try to escape. The others decide not to "provoke" the assailant because they assume that he is "only planning to rape them." The woman then hides under a bed. She lives to tell the tale. Her unfortunate roommates are rewarded for their compliance by being murdered one by one.

Let us now tell you that this unlikely story line actually happened. The year was 1966, the city was Chicago, the women were all student nurses, and the itinerant murderer was Richard Speck. There are so many strategies that could have been used to avert these tragic events. Consider the numerous options that were available to these women as the tale unfolded. Also consider the impossibility of a role-reversal situation occurring in which one female overcomes nine males. Can you imagine one woman subduing and systematically murdering eight physically healthy young men? Never! And yet the reverse is true.

Summary

In this chapter we have discussed fourteen dangerous situations that are commonly encountered. You should be able to imagine more situations applicable to you. Do so. Such mental preparedness is your best means of implementing the first two principles of personal defense: Eliminate dangers, and recognize and avoid potential dangers.

Chapter 7
Protecting Children from Sexual Offenders

An Introduction

Every boy and girl is a potential victim for a child molester. The stereotyped victim, a pretty little girl with golden curls dressed in a pink pinafore, simply doesn't match the facts as shown by police reports. Boys are victims as frequently as girls, fat children as frequently as thin, and attractive ones as often as the homely.

Psychiatric studies of adults who sexually abuse children have revealed some of the reasons why any child could be attacked. A molester creates a script, or fantasy, in his or her mind of a drama that ends with the molester reaching an orgasm in the last act. In order to carry out this drama, the molester creates a stage, in real life, and places on it two characters, himself or herself and the child victim. The molester's fantasy and imagination take over and determine how the victim looks. The fantasy determines that what role the victim takes. The fantasy determines what role the victim will be forced to play and what actions to take. Thus the victim is but a faceless mannequin, a screen on which the sexual offender projects his or her sexual needs. Once the offender reaches sexual gratification, the grip of the compulsion loosens and reality sets in. It is at this point that the child victim is beaten, threatened, or bribed not to tell. In some instances the child is killed. We are all familiar with such tragedies. The widely publicized Atlanta Youth Murderer and the Los Angeles Freeway Killer both forced many child victims into homosexual acts and then killed them.

Individuals who use children to achieve sexual gratification may be quite normal socially, as well as sexually, when not in the grip of their sexual perversion. Unfortunately, they do not have a glazed look in their eyes and do not act weird when around children. In fact, they may be good parents, kindly uncles and aunts, loving brothers and sisters, or generous neighbors. Since a pervert could be hidden in one of these respectable roles, it places a large responsibility on parents. Yes, every child must be protected from these criminals who are so hard to identify.

When a child is sexually attacked by a relative, it is called incest; when attacked by a stranger, it is called child molestation. But whatever the name, it is the most hideous of crimes—a crime that leaves a lifelong scar on the mind of the child victim. Like any scar, its presence can be seen long after the wound has healed. As in the case of any attack, prevention is best; but having failed that, the way one treats child molestation plays a large part in determining how the child copes with life years later. In this chapter we shall stress the strategies of personal defense as well as how parents of a molested child should act to maintain the mental health of their child.

Parents' Responsibility

Eliminating Danger

Parental awareness is the level at which eliminating danger begins. Keep in mind that sexual satisfaction for uncounted thousands of perverts can only be achieved by using children as sexual objects. These perverts engage in direct genital contact with children, as if they were adults, or use the child as objects with which to masturbate. To restate our explanation, the pervert is acting out a scene from his or her own childhood and has cast the child victim to play a role in his or her grim drama. A typical example of such a person is provided from our records by the actual case of "Uncle Bob," who often volunteered to read bedtime stories to his niece. He did this until she was eight years old. He then volunteered to do the same for her younger sister who was just turning four. Shortly after he began playing kindly uncle to the four-year-old, she asked her mother, "Why did Uncle Bob put my hand between his legs and make funny noises?" Her horrified mother then discovered the sad fact that her otherwise "normal" brother Bob had been sexually abusing her older daughter for three years and had threatened her into not telling. His second niece, however, was not intimidated by his threats, and her curiosity led to his being discovered.

Recognizing and Avoiding Danger

Without a doubt, countless episodes of child molestation go unaccounted for because parents refuse to recognize that such things can happen to their children, particularly by apparently "normal" adults. If any child says that he or she has been sexually abused, we recommend that you take it seriously.

Making children aware of the fact that they can be sexually abused is the second step on the path to recognizing and avoiding danger. Modesty, respect for privacy, and stressing the fact that one's genitals should only be touched by doctors and nurses who have parental approval are lessons that a child must learn by age three or four.

The third step in recognizing and avoiding this danger is to create an atmosphere in which a victimized child feels comfortable enough to report the crime. Many parents, seen in consultation, have asked why their child did not tell them until he or she had been molested several times. The answer usually was found in an assessment of the parent-child relationship. Imagine how hard it would have been for you, as a nine- or ten-year-old, to discuss normal sexual matters with your parents. Then multiply that manyfold by the anxiety you would have had in discussing shameful, forbidden activity. A severe problem can arise when children tell their parents of being victimized and are ignored or made to feel that he or she contributed to the perverse act in some way. Such blaming, directly or indirectly, can permanently damage the child just as much as the perverse act itself.

Children's Responsibility

Eliminating Danger

We recommend that families discuss such things as sexual attacks on children when they are reported on the news or otherwise come up in the course of daily conversation. This will help eliminate the stigma attached to such subjects. We have little hesitancy in conducting fire drills in school with children; in fact, we have them by law. In a similar vein you should forewarn your children by holding "perversion drills" and

prepare them. Perversion drills should consist of family discussions that
cover the following topics.

1. Children must be informed that there are people who will want to
   use their bodies for "naughty, illegal, unhealthy practices."
2. These people will act normal and appear friendly.
3. They will try to get the child to go with them on foot or in a car.

Your child should be firmly instructed that he or she should *never,
never, never* go with a stranger *no matter what his or her story* may be.
Some child molesters lure children by dressing in police uniforms, some
by loitering at parks and schools for weeks at a time to target their victims,
while others simply attempt bribery or use force. Let us reiterate, there are
no personal characteristics or common denominators of molesters that
could forewarn a child—only their actions. Thus any action by a stranger
to get the child alone must be taken as evidence by the child that the
person is to be feared. In this case fear is appropriate and can be life-
saving.

A fun and easy way to teach children to eliminate danger is called
role playing. In this technique a potentially dangerous situation is created
and a brief script of what could happen is discussed. Then each partici-
pant acts out each part of the script. For example, mother pretends that
she is a stranger trying to get Johnny, her seven-year-old son, into her car.
Next, Johnny pretends that he is the potential molester and tries to lure his
mother, the potential victim, into his car. By having the child assume both
roles he better understands the motives of the assailant, the nature of the
danger, and what he should do.

Recognizing and Avoiding Danger

Equipped with the foreknowledge that perverts exist and that children should never go anywhere with strangers, they should then be instructed to react properly when approached by a potential molester. The
proper response when approached by a stranger is to maintain distance,
politely answer a nonpersonal question such as a direction, and avoid
further conversation. Reject offers of rides, candy, or other enticements.
Successful bribes that have led to child molestation include: "I have some
baby puppies at home that you can play with," "Would you like to ride
my pony?" "I live right across the street and have just bought a chocolate
cake that you can have," "Your mother asked me to drive you home."
Corny as these ploys may sound, they have actually been reported by
traumatized victims.

Your instructions to your children on recognizing these dangers are
simple: Scream "fire, fire" and run to safety. Safety in this case is where
there are other people—run into a store, gas station, or home, if it is near.

Fighting

Since children's levels of maturity and physical capacity are so varied, we are unable to give you specific recommendations for fighting techniques. Opinions vary widely on this subject with some experts suggesting that children, once in the clutches of an assailant, should be as cooperative as possible. Others advocate teaching children to fight. Your own common sense is the best guide to determine what to teach your children. Take into account these factors: emotional maturity, size, aggressiveness, physical coordination, and levelheadedness under stress. If you decide to instruct your child to fight, emphasize that the element of surprise will be his or her greatest asset. The first attack must gain the child his or her freedom and not just anger the assailant. In other words, the first round is probably the only bout in this fight.

Incest

Incest, sexual activity between close family members, is referred to by psychiatrists as "the unspoken crime." This label comes from the fact that most victims of incest refused to report the crime when they were children. In therapy, as adults, they confess how they were torn within themselves to expose one parent to another because the parent may then be put in jail or forced to move out of the house. Often the victim carries the burden of guilt, blaming himself or herself for the sexual assaults.

Incest is frequent. We cannot cite accurate statistics because most instances of incest are unreported. Incest occurs in all social classes, races, and religions and takes many forms. Some less obvious examples are: a mother who continues to bathe her son until he is in his late teens and who "washes his genitals thoroughly to ensure that they are clean"; a mother who showers with her daughter and insists they cleanse each others genitals, which produces mutual orgasm; a father who kisses his daughter goodnight while pressing his penis against her to arouse himself; brothers and sisters who share the same bed during puberty and engage in masturbation and intercourse. These subtle forms of incest are just as damaging to the victim as the obvious form of genital intercourse between mother and son or father and daughter.

How can you determine if your child is a victim of incest? Unfortunately, no simple guidelines exist. As with any psychic trauma, certain symptoms can alert you. A child who suddenly avoids wanting to be left in the care of a certain relative, a child who suddenly insists on the presence of a trusted person at bedtime, or a child who regresses and acts in an infantile manner may be expressing anxieties caused by incestuous activities. Other possible symptoms are discussed in the next section.

Minimizing Psychological Damages Caused by Sexual Abuse

Even a child who has been forewarned and acted prudently may be abducted and molested. Sensitivity and proper reactions on the part of parents can minimize the psychological damage and longrange detrimental effects in children who have been molested. Like physical injuries, psychological bruises require time to heal. Parents should know that psychological healing goes through stages. First, one can expect the child to try to ignore or minimize what happened: "Oh, it was nothing and I've forgotten about it already." Days or weeks later the second phase occurs. Memories and painful feelings creep into consciousness with resulting anxiety and inappropriate reactions. Nightmares, fears apparently unrelated to the trauma, irritability, mood swings, and feelings of guilt over previously ignored actions occur. Specific psychological symptoms may arise. These include bedwetting, body twitches, phobias, obsessive thoughts, and school failure. At this point the child victim may either not associate these symptoms with the attack or blame himself or herself and thus suffer extraordinary guilt. If this stage or these symptoms persist for more than a month, professional help should be sought. A child psychiatrist, pediatrician, licensed clinical child psychologist, or child-guidance clinic can provide the necessary evaluation and treatment. We cannot stress how important it is to aid the healing process and make the child victim recover properly. Just as an unset bone may never be walked on again, so too can improperly healed psychological traumas cripple a child for life.

To foster this healing process, begin by creating an atmosphere in which the child can discuss, if he or she wishes, the events that took place. Neither insist that the child talk nor discourage him or her from doing so; rather, leave the door open. When unusual reactions or symptoms occur, be patient. Explain that they are to be expected, and predict that they will pass in time. Above all, let the child describe the trauma as many times as he or she wants, allowing psychological digestion to take place. Emphasize over and over again the child's lack of guilt or responsibility for what happened.

Reporting Child Molestations to the Police

The question of police intervention and prosecution must be faced squarely. We strongly advocate that all such crimes be reported and that every child victim participate completely with the police. This advice is based on sound principles of mental health as well as civic responsibility. It is helpful for the child to know that his or her parents, the police, and society are angry at the assailant, that the assailant has done wrong and should be punished, and that they all can be helpful in this process. Such arguments as "I won't prosecute because I don't want my child to go through all that," "The sooner we all forget it, the better," and "We want to avoid publicity" are often-heard spurious arguments. In fact, following such advice could be detrimental to the healing process. For example, not trying to prosecute might well encourage a child's natural sense of guilt to the point at which he or she then feels that others think he or she is guilty. After all, if he or she were innocent, there would be no qualms about going after the guilty person. This is how the mind of a child works. We can best teach our children that crime does not pay by having them aid us and the police in whatever steps are necessary to apprehend and punish their molesters. Even though the steps may take months or years, the end result will more than justify the means. Not pursuing justice can teach the sad lesson to children that crime can pay at their expense. Parents, too, can benefit by focusing their rage where it belongs—in seeking justice.

Chapter 8
Rape—Don't Take It Lying Down

The FBI Uniform Crime Report defines rape as "the carnal knowledge of a female forcibly and against her will." State statutes define the crime differently, but they all contain the common denominators of force and sexual contact.

What are your chances of being raped? Rape is the fastest growing crime against women, increasing at a rate of more than 10 percent per year. The incidence of rape is distributed evenly throughout the country, but a woman living in a city has a three-times greater chance of becoming a rape victim than her rural counterpart. These and any statistics on rape should not be taken at face value because as the FBI points out, "Rape is the most under-reported crime in the United States. This phenomenon is due primarily to a victim's fear of her assailant and her sense of embarrassment over the attack." Authorities surmise that only one in ten rapes is reported. Last year the FBI estimated that 76,250 forcible rapes occurred, or 210 per day. If one multiplies the reported rapes by ten, it is reasonable to assume that more than 2,000 rapes a day occur in the United States. This is a horrible, frightening statistic.

What happens to the rapists? Over half of them in "reported" crimes are never apprehended. If one takes account of unreported rapes, then we can assume that 95 percent of rapists are never caught. Of those few rapists arrested, 65 percent are prosecuted. Acquittals and dismissals resulted in 40 percent of these cases, and 47 percent are found guilty of rape, while 13 percent are convicted of lesser offenses. A sad conclusion can be drawn from these figures: Namely, a rapist has the favorable odds of getting away with his crime 99 times out of 100.

Further research reveals the following information concerning rapists. (Bear in mind that this research describes statistical norms.) It indicates that the "typical rapist" is an unskilled laborer, of low intelligence, eighteen years of age, unmarried, lacks confidence in his sexual capabilities, and is most likely to rape on a Saturday during the month of August between the hours of 8:00 P.M. and 2:00 A.M. Menachem Amier, in his study *Patterns in Forcible Rape*, points out that 76 percent of the rapists carefully plan their assaults and preselect their victim. The usual stereotype that the rapist simply "flips out" and impulsively attacks a victim is not true. Amier analyzed 646 cases and found that in 85 percent of the crimes physical force and/or weapons were used by the rapist. He also reported that 56 percent of the rapes occurred in the home, 18 percent occurred out of doors, and 15 percent in cars. Forty-eight percent of the rapists selected their victims from pedestrians. In characterizing rapists, he noted that 70 percent of them had prior records and 85 percent of these were repeat offenders.

Police reports indicate that when a man commits rape for the first time, the chances are 50–50 that he knows his victim. Thus your assailant may well be a man you know and have come to trust, such as an elevator operator, a deliveryman, or a fellow student.

Historical Background

Our current attitudes about rape have deep historical roots. During the Babylonian and Hebraic eras, men were the sole owners of property, and women were just one of their possessions. The value of a woman reflected the wealth and power of her owner (father), and her virginity was part of the bargaining price. Strict religious and civil laws determined how "female property" was protected and what happened to both the violators and property if damage to the goods occurred. For example, under Babylonian law girls were betrothed by their fathers when very young and lived with them until they married. After marriage they became the property of their husbands. At no time during their lives were they independent, nor did they live alone. If raped while living with her father, a woman was considered guiltless but remained "damaged goods." If married and raped, she was held accountable and punished along with her rapist. Both were thrown into a river to drown. If a husband chose to "forgive" his wife, he could jump into the river and save her. The rapist could be saved by the king's decree.

A detailed account of this history is provided by Susan Brownmiller in her informative book entitled *Against Our Will*. She traces how the Hebrews modified the Babylonian laws concerning rape. The Hebrews also viewed a daughter as property for the father to sell but shifted the responsibility for maintaining virginity to the woman. If a virgin were raped within the city, she was held accountable because she failed to scream loudly enough to have summoned help. Therefore both she and the rapist were stoned to death. If she were raped outside the city walls where her screams might have gone unheard, the rapist would have to pay the father fifty shekels and marry her. But if she were betrothed, the rapist was stoned to death, and the girl was unpunished and sold at a bargain-basement price by her dishonored father.

Another legacy of women being considered chattel can be found in Judeo-Christian postwar behavior. Women's bodies were considered by our victorious ancestors as bounty, to be taken, used, and discarded as befit the whims of the victors. From the earliest prebiblical accounts up to and including our most recent war, soldiers raped conquered women. This served many purposes including further defamation of the conquered males, degradation of the conquered females, and release of the warrior's pent-up emotions during battle. Conquered women also provided a source of slave labor, concubines, and breeding stock for their conquerors. Sad to say, such practices by conquering armies continue even today, attesting to the immutability of these attitudes handed down by our forebears.

Misconceptions About Rape

Because of the emotionally charged nature of the subject, many misconceptions exist about what takes place in the minds of rapists and their victims. For example, students have told us that their fathers and boyfriends believe that no woman can be forcibly raped because of anatomical reasons. Men also have told us that a woman has to voluntarily comply. Neither is true. There is no anatomical way a bound or threatened woman can prevent penetration.

Another common misconception is that "a woman can run faster with her skirt up than a rapist with his pants down." This witty but ridiculous statement was once made to me (Dr. Conroy) by no less an "authority" than a State of California judge. I was lecturing on rape, and he interrupted with his thoughtless statement. It is simply not true. Rare is the woman who can outrun a man. We have never heard of a rape that began with a woman holding her skirt up and a man hobbled with his belt and pants around his ankles.

Another common misconception, typical of male chauvinism, is that women secretly want to be raped. Psychological research has revealed, contrary to this belief, that women who actually want to be raped are rare. The belief that all women secretly harbor the desire may represent a projection of men's wishes. The vast majority of women abhor the thought of being forced into intercourse. One must carefully distinguish between normal, loving fantasies of seducing and being seduced from a neurotic desire to be forcefully raped. The former fantasies contain positive and loving elements. The latter expresses perversion.

Another common misconception is that a rapist's primary goal is to achieve sexual gratification. Studies of rapists reveal, on the contrary, that they are usually preoccupied with assaulting and injuring. Most rapists don't care what their victims look like. The victim is simply an object, not a human being. Frequently, a rapist can't recall a single thing about his victim. Furthermore, psychological analysis of many rapists has revealed that their victims represented a substitute for someone in their past whom they hated but against whom they could not express their anger.

Still another common misconception is that any normal man, given the proper set of circumstances, can be "enticed" into raping. There is simply no evidence to indicate that this is true. A normal man could no more be "enticed" into raping a scantily clothed woman than he could be "enticed" into stealing an expensive diamond necklace from a jewelry store or a Mercedes from an automobile showroom. Women are no more responsible for being raped than are jewels and cars responsible for being stolen. A connection between a woman's attire and sexual arousal leading to rape was drawn by Wisconsin Dane County Judge Archie Simonson. While presiding over a case involving a sixteen-year-old girl who was raped by three boys in a stairwell of their high school. Simonson stated that the rape had been the boys' "normal reaction" to sexual permissiveness and provocative clothing. The victim was wearing jeans, a turtleneck sweater, and an overblouse. (That's provocative, Archie?) He continued his unrealistic tirade by adding "I'm trying to say to women, stop teasing." Fortunately, the angry outcry to this exercise in judicial chauvinism led to a recall election that removed Simonson from his post.

To further demonstrate that a judicial comment is not necessarily a judicious one, look at the example of Connecticut Common Pleas Court Judge Walter Pickett. Judge Pickett was presiding over an abduction-rape case in which one of the four assailants was unable to get an erection. Pickett ordered that he not be bound over for trial, adding "You can't blame somebody for trying." The implicit or unspoken assumption that women are responsible for being raped led to this ridiculous suggestion several years ago in the Israeli parliament: To curb the increasing number of rapes in Tel Aviv, it was proposed that women be outlawed from the streets after dark. Prime Minister Golda Meir said of this proposal: "A curfew for women? Women aren't committing rape. Have a curfew for men."

Another myth is that women "cry rape" when it actually has not occurred. A recent study by the New York City Police Department exploded this myth. They found that the false-report rate for rape was only 2 percent, which is equivalent to the false-report rate for other felonies.

Another misconception is that if a victim seriously injures a rapist, the victim may be prosecuted and sent to jail. A UPI article published June 7, 1979, in the *Los Angeles Times* dispels that concern: "The Maine Supreme Court has upheld the right to use deadly force to repel a sexual attack." The article reported that Leland B. Philbrick of Old Town, Maine, successfully repelled the sexual attack of Charles Porterfield of Cape Elizabeth by shooting him to death. "In its decision, the court affirmed a state law that allows someone to repel a person trying to commit a forcible sex offense, even if it results in death." Although the wording of the law may vary from state to state, the law is the same.

The misconceptions we shall disclose concerning rape are: *Myth:* Rapists select strangers as victims. *Fact:* More than 50 percent of the victims are known. *Myth:* Rape is a crime of impulse. *Fact:* The majority of rapes are planned in advance. *Myth:* Most rapists are sex-crazed perverts. *Fact:* Most rapists lead normal heterosexual lives and have ample opportunity for sexual relations. *Myth:* Most rapes occur in dark alleys. *Fact:* More than 50 percent of all rapes occur in homes. *Myth:* Black men rape white women. *Fact:* Rapist and victim are usually of the same race. *Myth:* Only "bad women" get raped. *Fact:* Anybody can be a victim, and social reputation is not a factor. The June 25, 1978, issue of *Family Weekly* reported "A rape-victim advocate center in Florida found that their youngest victim was two months, and oldest 85 years." *Myth:* Women cannot protect themselves from rapists. *Fact:* There is no question that women with proper psychological preparation and practical methods of self-defense can prevent and indeed have prevented rape.

Psychology of the Rapist

The possibility of being raped exists for every woman regardless of how pretty, how plain, how young, or how old she is. Psychiatric studies of known rapists reveal that they performed this type of crime for many different reasons. Although it is difficult to make generalizations about what a "typical rapist" is like, we present the following.

The Psychotic

One common type of rapist is the psychotic, or severely deranged man, who seeks sexual contact in order to act out his delusions. This type of man may be convinced that you are or he is someone else because of his severe mental illness. He uses the threat of force to get you to participate in his delusions.

The causes of such severe psychological disturbances are many. Schizophrenia and manic psychosis are common illnesses that can produce such delusional behavior. Other causes include temporary insanity induced by the effects of drugs on the brain. Such drugs include alcohol, LSD, PCP (Angel Dust), and speed (amphetamines). Delusional men often can appear to be sane and rational, and the stereotype of the glassy-eyed, wildly talking, "crazy" rapist does not hold. Thus there are no easy guidelines that we can offer you for making an on-the-spot "diagnosis." However, the more bizarre his request, the more unrealistic his suggestions, and the more confused he appears to be, the more likely it is that he is psychotic. When you are faced by a psychotic rapist, our general guidelines still apply: Avoid danger by talking agreeably to him, do not contradict his delusions, never confront him with his craziness, and only attack if your life or health is directly threatened.

Alcohol is probably the most common cause of temporary psychosis, and there are many examples of assaults on women by drunk men who would not have behaved in such a manner if sober. We know of a recent court case in which a man went to a neighborhood bar following an argument with his wife and began an innocent conversation with a woman there. She was sympathetic to his complaints about his wife and did not realize that he was drunk. She unwisely agreed to let him drive her home. He attempted to rape her in the parking lot. Fortunately her screams attracted other patrons from the bar who summoned police. The man was quite chagrined when he sobered up and had no recollection of his behavior.

An example of severe psychotic illness leading to murder was the sensational Son of Sam case in New York City. The young man in this case heard the voice of a dog ordering him to shoot young women with a .44 caliber revolver. Psychiatric evaluation after his arrest determined that he suffered from schizophrenia and acted on the basis of psychotic delusions. Psychotic illnesses leading to rape have been portrayed in countless movies and television shows. In many of these scripts, the psychotic lures his victim into a situation in which she must play out the role of the attacker's girl friend, mother, or a prostitute. These are rare occurrences.

The Pervert

Another type of rapist is the sexual pervert. This man weaves elaborate fantasies about specific women with whom he wishes to practice sadistic sexual acts. When these fantasies become overwhelming or are given unwitting encouragement by a naive women, he rapes her.

An example of this was recently related by a reader. For two years she had been acquainted with a middle-aged, married man who lived in her apartment building. She was also friendly with his wife and considered them to be a happily married couple. On several occasions she had seen the man zipping up his fly in the hallway and in the garage. She had paid no attention to these apparently disconnected and harmless incidents. One evening she met him by chance on the elevator. He asked if she had a spare light bulb that he could borrow. Thinking this was an innocent request, she invited him to wait in her living room while she looked for one. When she returned to the living room, light bulb in hand, she was horrified to see him standing with his genitals exposed. He pleaded with her to have sexual relations. He said he had exposed himself many times to her before and was sure she liked to look at him. He had staged their meeting tonight, lied about the light bulb, and would not leave until he was satisfied.

The Opportunist

This kind of rapist misinterprets your friendly smile, gesture, or innocent conversation to the point at which he believes you are willing to have sexual relations. When he reveals his intentions and you bring him back to reality, he becomes angry and threatens rape. We know of a young woman who was in the habit of hitchhiking. One day she accepted a ride from a well-groomed man in an expensive car. She chatted amiably with him and noticed too late that he was driving into a deserted area behind a warehouse. He was arrested after attempting to rape her. His story was that she had been "very friendly and coming on strong," that "she was braless and exposed her thighs by raising her skirt." He felt "seduced." She felt that she had not been acting in a seductive manner, that she was only concerned about arriving at her destination safely, and was completely surprised when he suddenly stopped the car and told her to have sexual relations with him. When she refused, he called her a tease, ripped her blouse open, and pinned her against the car door. Fortunately, there were people emerging from the warehouse, and her screams attracted their attention as she struggled to flee from the car. The marked contrast between the ways the man and the woman viewed this situation must be emphasized. The woman viewed hitchhiking as an inexpensive way of getting home. She was dressed in a manner typical of women in her age group. To the man, she looked and acted like a "pickup" who was advertising "I am available." The way the "opportunist" rapist sees a woman is filtered through his emotions and desires and has little to do with the way you may see yourself.

Strategies for Dealing with Rape

A woman threatened with rape faces the possibility of losing her life. Tragically, women have been murdered because they resisted a rapist when otherwise they might have lived if they had complied. We agree with the saying "It's better to lose your virginity than your life." Unfortunately, following this advice will not guarantee safety. Some rapists murder their submissive victims. However, research indicates that most rapists release their victims once they have satisfied their sadistic needs. Brownmiller speculates that approximately 2 percent of all murder victims are raped and only 2 percent of all rapes or attempted rapes are rape-murders. Therefore fewer than two women are murdered out of every thousand who are raped. In any event, our advice is to fight when you are in immediate danger of your life or bodily harm and there is no possible way to talk your way out of the situation or to flee.

The following are true accounts of women who have talked their way out of being raped. A recent student of ours had just completed jury duty and related the following fascinating case to us. She described how a young woman used her wits to escape from two kidnappers who threatened her with rape. Her trauma began while walking home from school. A van pulled up at the curb beside her and a well-groomed young man got out to ask directions. Then, he said, "I'm not sure I understand. Will you please explain this to the driver?" As she leaned into the open door where a map was spread on the passengers' seat, she was shoved inside the van. In a split second the door slammed, and the van sped off.

"We've been watching you, baby. We like the way you walk, and we're going to have a party you'll never forget," said the driver while his accomplice menaced her with a switchblade knife.

Our student then told the class that this clever woman said the most amazing thing. "Look, you guys, I really dig your macho style. My girl friend, Jill, and I turn on to this kind of action." She backed up her words with a smile and caressed the driver's knee. She proceeded to give a vivid description of her make-believe friend's body and crazed sexual appetites. She then gave directions to Jill's house, which in fact was where her older brother lived with three other men. When they arrived she volunteered to get Jill, but they insisted on accompanying her to the door. When her brother answered the door, she bolted inside screaming. Her brother and his roommates subdued the assailants, who were brought to trial and actually convicted for kidnap and attempted rape. Let us stress that in this true story a victim was able to save her life, avoid rape, and convict her assailants without fighting.

Our second true story is of a housewife who lived near the site of some construction work. One hot, sunny day, a construction worker, who she noted had been smiling at her, suddenly appeared at her door. He asked if he might come in for a drink of water because their supply had run out at the construction site. Having seen the man at work for several weeks, she was not suspicious and decided to be neighborly. Once inside, however, her mistake became all too clear when he roughly shoved her into the bedroom and lifted her skirt. Thinking quickly she relaxed her body and said as calmly as possible, "Please hurry. My husband and a couple of his bowling-team friends will be here any minute. I'm supposed to have cold beer and sandwiches ready. He'll kill us both if he finds us this way." As she hoped, the man released her and fled. Needless to say, her husband was not on his way home. He didn't even own a bowling ball. She called the police, and the assailant was arrested at work.

Our last true story concerns a waitress who also pretended to cooperate with her assailant. She was awakened in her bed by an intruder who entered through her second-story bathroom window. He threatened her with an ice pick as he undressed. "Look, this is okay with me, but I don't want to get pregnant. My diaphragm is in the bathroom, and it will only take a second to insert it." As she had hoped, he agreed to let her get up and go into the bathroom. She left the door ajar so as not to arouse suspicion, turned on the water to cover any sounds, and fled naked through the window. Now, the unbelievable part of the tale: She called the police from her neighbor's house. They arrived promptly and found her would-be rapist lying naked on her bed, eager with anticipation.

The common denominators in these successful escapes are that the victims acted calmly, cooperated with their assailants, and pretended to surrender. Thus their assailants let their guard down initially, and the women gained time to plan their escapes. These women were fortunate in that they were able to talk to their assailants and the men responded somewhat sanely. Other assailants are more intent on gaining release of their hostility and anger toward women, and the promise of cooperation and sexual release does not interest them.

When talking to a rapist fails and there is no way to flee, your tactics may or may not include fighting. Your decision to fight is based on an assessment of the following factors: (1) How many assailants are present? (2) Are weapons present? How lethal are they? Where are they? (3) What bodily weapons are available to you and which vulnerable areas can you strike? and (4) How and where will you flee?

Here are three situations in which talking has failed and the decision to submit or to fight must be made. Our first hypothetical victim, Judy, while waiting at a well-lighted bus stop one evening, suddenly feels a muscular arm around her neck, lifting her from her feet and dragging her into the bushes. She feels herself being thrown to the ground, and a man falls on her. She catches a glimpse of his angry eyes and smells alcohol and sweat. "You will die, but if you shut up and don't struggle, I'll kill you quick. Otherwise, you'll suffer." Let us interrupt this narrative to point out the following: (1) Judy has no way to talk or flee. (2) Her life is threatened by an irrational assailant. (3) Physical assault has commenced and requires a life-saving counterattack. Meanwhile, back in the bushes, Judy instinctively knows that her best tactic is the thumb gouge. As her assailant tears at her blouse, she screams while thrusting her thumbs into his eyes. She then rolls him off her body, springs to her feet, and immobilizes him with kicks to his head. She then flees for help screaming "fire, fire."

Our second hypothetical victim, Sarah, has no choice but to succumb to rape in an attempt to save her life. She is walking home from work in a familiar neighborhood on a familiar street. She has little cause to be concerned because it is midafternoon and there are other pedestrians within sight. A car pulls alongside, and a husky voice calls out, "Hey lady, where's the police station in this neighborhood?" As she turns to answer, she sees that the car has stopped, both doors have swung open, and three young thugs are leaping out at her. She instinctively tries to scream and run. Her scream is stifled by a hand across her mouth, while another pair of hands picks her up by the waist, and a third pair lifts her knees. The next thing she hears is the slamming of the car doors and the laughing of the four thugs as the car lurches forward. The kidnappers begin arguing over who will rape her first, and one of them ties a handkerchief over her eyes. The man holding her mouth whispers, "All we want is a little fun, baby; cooperate with us and you won't get hurt." At this point Sarah must decide which tactics are best. Her life is not in immediate danger. As long as she remains blindfolded, she believes that they will not have to kill her to avoid identification. On the other hand, it is unlikely that she could fight off four strong men and attempting to do so might aggravate them into hurting her more. Her only tactic is to try to remain calm, prepare herself to endure multiple rapes, do nothing to provoke further physical assault, and gather data in order to identify them. Many rape victims in similar situations have cooperated and were released without physical injury. To conclude our story, Sarah's rapists left her blindfolded, bound, and gagged but alive.

Our third hypothetical victim, Margarita, is confronted with another type of attack. Her first glimpse of the assailant is over a gun that is thrust in her face. The words she hears are "Do what I say or I'll kill you." She follows his directions and enters his car. At gunpoint he forces her to drive to an isolated area. Throughout the drive she maintains a conversation with him, trying to sound calm and cooperative. All the while she is mentally preparing herself for the possibility that he will put his gun down. If he does, she knows that her chance to fight will have arrived. Should she gouge his eyes or pull his groin? What follow-through techniques will she use to immobilize him? And how best to flee? These are questions she mulls over. "Pull over in that field 'cause I'm gonna give it to you there." As the car comes to a stop, he places the gun under the seat and reaches for his zipper. Her moment to attack has arrived. Margarita's hands fly from the wheel to the sides of his head, and her thumbs gouge into his eyes. Terrified, his hands grasp for his blinded eyes and his head pitches forward in pain, exposing his neck. She easily delivers a double-hand blow to the base of his skull. Blinded, stunned, and racked with pain, he is helpless. She stretches toward the door handle on his side, unlatches it, and by leaning against her door thrusts him out of the car with her feet. Not stopping to close the door, she drives off to freedom.

Lest you mistakenly think that by fighting back you will increase the chance of getting hurt, let us cite the following. A report from the Denver Anti-Crime Council noted that of 915 potential rapes that were studied 304 victims successfully resisted. Twenty-four percent of the victims fled to freedom, 18 percent fought back, and 15 percent drove the assailant away with screams. The study concluded that less than 9 percent of the women who resisted "sustained anything more serious than a scratch or bruise."

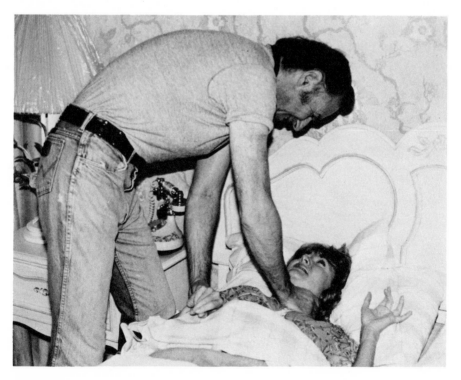

FIG. 8-1
DEFENSE AGAINST A RAPIST

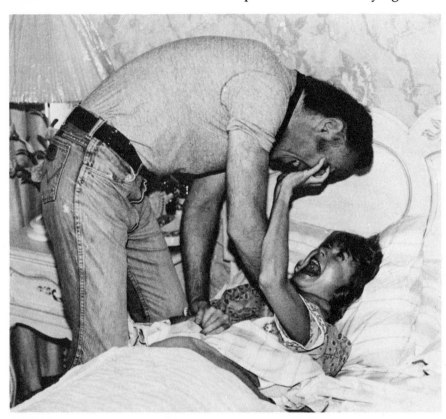

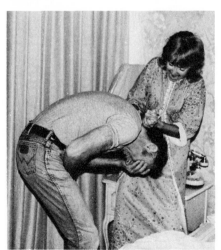 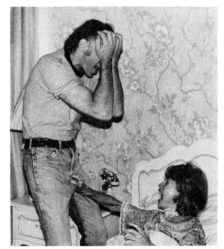

FIG. 8-1b, 8-1c, 8-1d (CONT'D)
DEFENSE AGAINST A RAPIST

Anatomy of a Rape

The following is a hypothetical sequence. We present it to help you visualize in slow motion what could transpire during an actual rape.

Stage 1: Rapist Selects Victim

Rapist, becoming overwhelmed with urges to act out aggressive fantasies, selects a victim. She must appear to be vulnerable—that is, distracted, preoccupied, infirm, intoxicated, or sleeping. A choice victim is friendly to strangers and appears to be helpful. *Victim* is not suspicious and lacks mental preparedness.

Stage 2: Rapist Contacts Victim

Rapist attempts to engage victim in conversation by asking for time of day or directions. *Victim* responds in a friendly and cooperative manner.

Stage 3: Rapist Gains Control of Victim

Rapist, using threats, intimidation, and possibly weapons, forces ►victim to cooperate. *Victim,* panicked by threats to her life, feels helpless and submits to control.

Stage 4: Physical Assault

Rapist tells victim what physical acts he desires. These are forms of sexual activity that will give the rapist an orgasm or other physical release. They may include vaginal, anal, or oral intercourse, being masturbated, masturbating while watching the victim, or beating the victim. *Victim,* terrorized into compliance, cooperates to the best of her ability in order to preserve her life.

Stage 5: Postrape

Rapist terminates the rape and with renewed threats tells victim not to scream, leave, or report him to the police. Some rapists apologize to their victims, while others may actually ask for future meetings. *Victim,* relieved to be alive, continues to cooperate until she is certain he is gone.

What to Do If Raped

Observe and Recall Details

Draw up a complete physical description of your assailant. Writing down details of what he did and said as soon as possible is helpful. Observe his direction of escape and by what means. If he leaves by car, try to note his license-plate number and the kind of car he is driving. Even a partial number can help the police in identifying a getaway car if the make and year are known. Keep any physical evidence he may have left behind, such as a weapon or a piece of clothing. To avoid destroying evidence, do not shower, douche, change your clothes, or clean up.

Immediately Notify the Police

State the following facts to the police telephone operator: your name, that you have been raped, and your exact location. Be prepared to answer questions on the phone about the description of your assailant and his weapon, if any, because the police will start looking for him immediately. Several women have told us that they were still so frightened when they first called that they could not bring themselves to describe the assailant. This need not happen to you if you are mentally prepared. The police will send an officer to assist you. In many states a female officer can be requested.

Call a Friend

While waiting for the police to arrive, you may find it helpful to telephone a mature and understanding friend or relative. If no one is available, phone the Rape Crisis Center in your district. They will try to send someone to help you.

Cooperate with Police Questioning

When the police arrive, answer all questions in detail. Do not assume that the police are accusing you. One woman, when asked about what clothing she was wearing, panicked because she thought the officer was implying that she had dressed in a manner that provoked the attack. It is the officer's job to obtain as much factual information as possible so that he or she can develop a picture of how the assailant operates and what type of women he seeks out. The facts about you could be helpful in this regard. You should also be prepared to answer specific questions about the exact nature of the assault. Discussing sexual activity, which in general is very difficult, can become almost impossible when you are standing on a street corner with your clothing disheveled and you are being queried by strangers in uniform. The police may ask you the same questions several times or from different points of view. Again, this is not to intimidate you but simply to help you recall what are painful but crucial events. One police officer said that he felt like a bull in a china shop when every question he asked only made a poor victim become more upset. Another officer confided that he camouflaged his feelings behind a "tough" facade because he was afraid of breaking down and crying with the battered victim.

Undergo Medical Examination

Next, be prepared emotionally to be examined by a physician who will detect injury as well as obtain evidence of rape admissible in court. The physician will perform a general physical examination and look for evidence of trauma. He or she will also perform a pelvic examination to determine if there are internal injuries and to obtain specimens. These specimens are studied to detect the presence of semen. Because of certain legal requirements, a police officer may have to be present during the examination, and a police photographer may be required to take pictures of bruises. This can be embarrassing if you are not emotionally prepared. The best preparation is to be forewarned and to remind yourself that you are helping the police to apprehend the man who attacked you. Because most venereal diseases have an incubation period of at least a week and pregnancy cannot be detected by tests for eleven to eighteen days after intercourse, you should also consult your family physician. Many states provide free postrape medical examinations.

We have been asked about the "morning after" pill, which is a hormone that can bring on a menstrual period at any time during the cycle. It is *not* a medication that is routinely administered. If someone recommends it to you or if you wish to take it yourself, we urge you to first consult a physician who is familiar with its use and side effects.

Following a rape or a similar traumatic experience, we recommend that victims stay with loved ones or friends and avoid being alone for a few days. We encourage them to talk about their experience rather than "try to forget it." Talking things out actually helps heal psychological scars. Attempting to reestablish a normal routine within a week or two is advisable.

Report to the Police Station

After you undergo medical examination, you will be asked to report to the police station and again give a detailed description of the attack. Expect to be quizzed with much repetition. Again, we remind you that the police are experienced in questioning victims who are under emotional stress. Try not to feel that they are being accusatory or threatening. They are only concerned with obtaining as many details as possible to further their chances of apprehending and convicting the rapist. Reviewing mug shots, cooperating with a police artist to form a composite picture, and restating the details of the attack are all routine procedures that you can expect. You will also be asked whether you would be willing to testify in open court. We encourage you to cooperate in every way possible—in every way that you feel is in keeping with your conscience and in every way that will help you heal the wounds that have been inflicted on you.

Take Legal Action

When your attacker is apprehended, you will be asked to identify him in a police lineup and to file specific charges against him. Many women have panicked at this prospect, resulting in the release of their rapists. If a woman does not press charges, the rapist is then given license to repeat his crime. Each municipality has its own prosecuting attorneys. They will contact you, reinterview you, and explain the procedures to you. Do not hesitate to ask questions while these legal steps are being taken. (See Taking Postattack Action on page 151.)

The most common defense that rapists' lawyers use is the following: "How could this handsome, well-groomed, intelligent young man [accompanied by his charming wife or loving girl friend] who has such an excellent school and work record and who attends church regularly be guilty of attacking this woman of obvious low moral character, etc., etc.?" It may be legally admissible to explore your past sexual behavior and other personality characteristics. Fortunately these laws are now changing, and women can look forward to better and equal treatment in the years ahead.

Postrape Reactions

From a psychiatric point of view, we consider rape a severe psychological trauma. It is an experience that must be emotionally dealt with and worked through. Research examining the reactions of rape victims indicates that they deal with rape in much the same way people react to other severe traumatic events such as death of a loved one, earthquakes, and terrorists' raids.

In the first stage of the "Rape Crisis Syndrome" the victim, confronting the reality of the immediate circumstances, experiences overwhelming panic, anxiety, numbness, loss of appetite, sleeplessness, nightmares, loss of normal energy levels, uncontrollable crying—or the inability to cry at all, and loss of memory recall. These reactions can last from hours to a few days and only gradually give way as the process of integrating the traumatic events begins. This is the phase when talking about what happened—to the police, to friends, and relatives—is particularly painful.

Next there usually comes a phase of self-doubt and guilt. The victim wonders to herself: "What did I do that this should have happened to me?" "How was I responsible?" "I wish I could have done something differently to recognize and avoid the attack," "Should I have fought rather than given in to save my life?" "Was my life actually threatened?" These feelings of self-doubt accompany underlying guilt. Victims must understand that it is not a crime to be raped. It is almost universal that such guilt is felt by a victim of rape or any other serious tragedy. In addition to the reactions listed above, typical reactions during this stage include depression, difficulties in intimate relationships, inability to cope with daily routines, impatience, and unusual displays of anger and fears of men, dying, being alone, and darkness. During this stage even an emotionally strong woman feels a sense of helplessness, loss, and lack of control over her life. Her inability to reason herself out of these feelings only adds to them. This stage usually lasts about four weeks.

The next phase usually is one in which anger surfaces and becomes focused on the assailant. "I should have killed him." "I hope the police find him and hang him from the highest tree." "I am going to buy a gun, find him myself, and shoot him." Such thoughts are all commonly heard from women at this stage of reaction, which usually lasts a few weeks. Throughout all three stages, the rape will be the primary thought in a victim's mind.

The final phase of reaction, called resolution, can last from six months to over a year. During this phase the woman becomes increasingly able to think back over the traumatic situation with lessening emotion. She gains perspective and accepts the fact that many things will happen in her life over which she has no control, and she acknowledges that these events are best left in the past. The victim begins to realize that spending emotional effort on such past events is useless and that it's better to count one's blessings and proceed with the business of life. During this resolution phase there will be echoes of past emotions, usually expressed as crying spells, nightmares, or sudden feelings of panic when something reminds her of the attack. For example, the "anniversary syndrome" is commonly experienced. This psychiatric term refers to a victim's reexperiencing painful emotions in the neighborhood in which a trauma occurred, when the same hour of the same day of the week comes around, or when the same time of the year arrives. These anniversary reactions are normal and represent the psychological work of integrating traumatic experience in a healthy way. Knowing what is normal is in and of itself helpful, and we have counseled many women who have benefited from understanding this simple point.

Sexual activity after a rape is difficult for the victim, and this too is to be expected. It will remind her of the degrading and life-threatening experience that accompanied the attack. We counsel the partners of rape victims to understand that it may take months for their loved ones to regain the capacity to enjoy sexual relations. In some cases husbands of rape victims also suffer intense, long-term psychological damage. Many men who can accept divorce and even infidelity cannot accept the rape of a wife. A sad statistic that demonstrates rape's traumatic effect on couples is that more than 50 percent of the relationships between husbands and wives and women and lovers are shattered within one year of the rape.

It is possible for a victim to lessen the emotional effects of rape and to shorten her recovery time. She can learn to deal with her problem. She does not have to continue to be a suffering victim. We are often asked if psychiatric consultation or psychotherapy is indicated for rape victims. Studies show that immediate crisis counseling greatly assists the victim as well as her loved ones. When counseling is needed, we recommend that a victim and her family seek help from her physician, a mental-health professional, or a community mental-health clinic.

Postrape counseling clinics, such as the Rape Crisis Center, have been established throughout the country. Their purpose is to provide rape victims with information and to refer them to the proper agencies for both medical and legal assistance. It is hoped that more of these centers will be established in the years ahead. Many of the counselors are rape victims themselves who speak from firsthand experience. We encourage women who have been physically assaulted, whether actually raped or not, to contact rape centers. If a center is not available in a victim's hometown, we suggest to her that it is well worth the price of a long-distance call. The directory-assistance operator in any large city will have the number readily available.

A True Experience

Only a woman who has been raped knows the horror and the lingering damage of this assault, and so we searched our files for the most vivid account to include in this chapter. The following description is in the words of Carolyn Craver, a San Francisco reporter. She was attacked on January 14, 1978, by a Berkeley rapist known as Stinky, who broke into her house through her six-year-old son's bedroom window and raped her for three hours. Editor Alison Wells reported her story in the quarterly journal *Self Determination*, volume II, issue II, 1978.

There was still something about me that believed that rape not only happened to other women, but it happened to another kind of woman. What ever that meant. It was something that just wouldn't happen to me.

I turned off the lights about midnight. The next thing I knew, I saw the dark image of a man flying at me covering my face with a gloved hand and pinning my arms down with his knees, he had one arm free, and with his other arm he stuck a knife at my throat and told me that if I said a word or did anything, he'd kill me.

I could feel him putting a cloth over my eyes, and he was covering my mouth with his hand, so I could neither yell nor bite him. He took his knife and cut my hand.

It was at that point that I heard my son yelling outside my bedroom door. He ordered me to tell my son to go back to bed. He said, "If your son comes in the room, I'll kill him." My terror was my son. I just felt as though I couldn't risk a thing. The thought of anything happening to my son . . . and the horrible fear that there was nothing I could do to protect him were overwhelming.

He started asking me about money, and then for a fleeting moment I thought maybe I'll get away with just being robbed. But when I told him my purse was in the living room, he clearly was not interested in getting it. I had on a floor-length nightgown, and that's when he pulled the nightgown up over my neck and, for the next two and a half to three hours, raped me.

I was terrified. I was absolutely terrified. He had a knife. Every few minutes, if I got to the point where I thought, "Well, maybe I can do something," he'd pick up the knife and stick it at my neck, or he'd stick it at my throat, to remind me that he had it.

He was constantly giving me orders, "Turn on your back; turn on your stomach." He turned me upside down in the bed and committed sodomy.

I was conscious that sex was really a minimal concern of his, that what he was really happy about was my terror and his dominance of me. The sex part of it—although it went on and on and on—was horrible. He was getting off on the terror and on violating me in whatever way he could.

"Now, if you do everything I say, I'll leave you the way I found you." He then took me to my son's door, which was open, and said, "It was good, wasn't it?" He told me to wait fifteen minutes before coming out. "Don't call the police or I'll come back and kill you and your son." I got the bedroom door closed, and I could hear him in the house. So, for a while I didn't do anything, just stood at the door.

Finally, I didn't hear anything. I called out, "Is anyone there?" No answer. Called out again, "Is anyone there?" I think I counted to twenty. I ran from my bedroom and I could see the living room window open. I ran and I turned on all the lights in the house.

One of the things about rape that's so horrible is the effect that it has on other people. Reporters always talk to rape victims, we don't talk to their families and their loved ones. My twin sister getting a phone call from the Berkeley police at five o'clock in the morning telling her that her sister's just been raped had to have been one of the worst things in the world for her. She couldn't believe it.

I wanted to talk about it. I felt that people really didn't know how horrible rape was. That for all my interviews, for all the other interviews that people had done with rape victims, that people had always been given a sanitized version of what rape was about. And it's really horrible. Short of like being killed, I don't know anything else that could happen to me that could be worse. And I wanted people to know how horrible it was.

Women get blamed for rape, and you know, it's always the victim, and I kept thinking that when somebody robs a bank, nobody goes up to the bank teller and says, "If you hadn't had a sign hanging outside, the guy wouldn't have known there was money inside, and he wouldn't have come in and robbed you." Nobody ever says to a banker on a witness stand, "Did you have illicit practices in your bank that somehow justified having your bank robbed?" No other victims in the world are treated the way rape victims are treated. Although I wasn't being treated that way—I was being treated with absolute respect and kindness by the Berkeley Police Department—it just made me furious to think of the other stories I had heard and knew about.

I think that there are lots of ways in which women can end their own victimization. One of them is by going to the police, and I feel real strongly about this. I think every woman who is raped must tell the police. I'll just kick somebody's teeth in who tells me, "Yeah, but the treatment I got from the police was as bad as getting raped." It is not. No matter what the police do, no matter how the prosecutors may handle it, no matter what the defense attorneys may do, it's not as bad. I can always tell somebody to shut up. To not report it to the police means to not do everything in your power to get the man who raped you behind bars; it means that you left an open invitation for that man. . . . You've said to your rapist, "Not only can you rape me, but you can rape anybody 'cause I ain't going to do anything about it and that shows you how vulnerable women are, and how we're totally your victims because we're not going to do anything about the fact that you raped us."

A woman who was raped by Stinky and did not report it to the police I consider almost as responsible for my rape as Stinky himself, because if there is a victim out there who has not reported it to the police, she may have information that could have led to his being captured and she left it open for me to become a victim. I don't give a damn what the circumstances were. You report being raped. You have to. It's an open invitation for that man to go out and rape somebody else. How could any woman . . . how could you conceivably leave that open to somebody else? to another sister? It's a crime you wouldn't wish on your worst enemy.

Talking about it, talking about it to any jerk who would listen has helped. And let me say that by talking about it, I don't mean just giving interviews and talking on television, I mean if people would sit and talk to me for three minutes on an airplane, I'd tell them I was a rape victim. I think talking has really made it better. It stopped it from becoming a nightmare. It's real. I'm a rape victim. I was raped. No matter what I think, no matter what I do, somebody broke into my house in the middle of the night and raped me. I think that one of the things that happens to women who don't talk about it is that it becomes a nightmare, it becomes this personal, secret, horrible night-

mare. They really live with some fears that I don't have to live with
. . . the anger, the hurt, the just incredible sense of violation.

A Success Story

It was a warm, sunny Tuesday in August of 1981. Lynn O'Donnell, age twenty-eight, of San Francisco and her friend Kathie Test, thirty-one, of New York City, both television producers, were picnicking on the Point Reyes Peninsula in northern California. According to their police affidavit, an armed gunman approached them and demanded their money. They complied but the man returned their wallets and forced them to walk to a secluded area.

He then ordered them to lie face down on the ground saying that he would kill Ms. O'Donnell if she moved. Ms. O'Donnell reported that she could feel the rifle barrel resting on her back and both of the man's hands on her left wrist as he attempted to tie her with a cord.

She decided to react. With her right hand Ms. O'Donnell grabbed the rifle barrel, twisted it, and fired point-blank at his stomach. The gun misfired. Her quick-thinking companion picked up a wine bottle and hit the assailant on the head. Following through, they broke the gun barrel over his head, kicked him in the groin, smashed his glasses, and ran for help.

Leonard Frank Tate, age thirty-six, of West Covina, California, the alleged assailant, was arrested several days later. His head was badly battered, his left hand was broken, and his left leg was seriously injured. Mr. Tate had served three sentences in state prison for burglary. He also has a record of arrests for kidnapping and assault.

The victims were praised by Sheriff Al Howenstein of the Marin Sheriff's Department for waiting for the proper moment to counterattack their assailant and for "using their heads."

By following the Conroy Method of Self-defense, you too can, if attacked, become a success story.

Chapter 9
Help the Police to Help You

Despite stereotypes to the contrary, the vast majority of law-enforcement personnel are intelligent, efficient, and dedicated men and women who are devoted to ensuring your safety. Much ignorance concerning police practices exists, which is perhaps why many crimes go unreported and, according to Walter Berns, resident scholar of the American Enterprise Institute for Public Policy Research, in his book *For Capital Punishment*, 97.5 percent of the criminals in the United States today are never caught. In this chapter we explain in detail what you can expect when you report a crime to the police. This information will make you more comfortable in the event that you have to report a crime.

Describing the Assailant

Ideally, every crime should be reported immediately after it has occurred. The sooner the police have information, the sooner they can apprehend your assailant. A general description of the assault and the assailant's physical characteristics, clothing, speech, accent, and words as well as how he approached and how he escaped must be told at once. By being observant during an encounter, you will gather the proper facts. (See Figure 9–1.) The police request the following information on all assailants.

Amputee

Leg	Ear	Foot
Arm	Fingers	Hand

Deformed
Leg
Arm
Hand
Limp
Fingers
Bowlegged
Tattoo
Arm
Hand
Fingers
Chest Neck
Pictures
Designs
Names
Words
Initials
Facial Scars
Cheek
Chin
Forehead
Lip
Nose
Ear
Eyebrow
Facial Oddities
Birthmarks
Pockmarks
Moles
Freckles
Pimples
Lips—Thick
Lips—Thin
Chin—Protruded
Chin—Receding
Hollow Cheek
Teeth
Missing
Gold
Broken
False
Stain/Decay
Protruding
Irregular

Body Scars
Arm
Hand
Wrist
Neck
Burn
Chest
Speech
Impediment
Accent (U.S.)
Accent (Other)
Lisps
Stutters
Harelip
Mumbles
Rapid
Soft/Low
Refined
Eyes
Missing
Crossed
Sunglasses
Glasses (Plain)
Bulging
Squint/Blink
Slanted
Hair Type
Dyed
Processed
Wig/Toupee
Crew Cut
Bald
Afro
Long
Thin/Receded
Straight
Wavy
Bushy
Curly
Facial Hair
Mustache-Chinese
Goatee
Beard-Full
Mustache-Heavy

Mustache-Medium
Mustache-Thin
Brows-Heavy
Unshaven
Ears
Cauliflower
Pierced
Protruding
Close to Head
Large
Small
Nose
Crooked
Hooked
Upturned
Long
Broad
Flat
Small
Thin
Face
Negro W/Cauc.
Features
High Cheek Bone
Long
Broad
Thin
Round
Complexion
Dark
Sallow
Ruddy
Light/Fair
Medium

FIG. 9-1   DESCRIBING THE ASSAILANT

Taking Postattack Action

If valuables were stolen, a complete listing of them is required. If personal injury occurred, you will be advised to seek medical attention. We urge you to follow this advice because anxiety and panic often cause the victim to ignore severe injuries. You may be requested to look through "mug shot" books in order to identify your assailant. These books are organized for easy identification of known criminals; they are grouped according to such criteria as age, sex, ethnic background, type of crime, and method of operation (M.O.). If identification cannot be made from mug shots, an artist may draw a composite picture of your assailant from your description. Very specialized techniques exist to aid artists in composing such pictures, and remarkably accurate representation can be made.

Once a suspect is apprehended, you can expect to be asked to identify him in a lineup. Your own identity will be protected at this point. If positive identification is made, the suspect will be formally arrested, booked, and may be allowed to post bail. At his arraignment the accused is formally charged with the offense, a trial date is set, and legal counsel obtained. The district attorney's prosecuting officer will represent you and advise you about your participation in the trial. You are not charged for this service, because the local law-enforcement agencies are responsible for prosecuting these types of crimes on citizens. When your case comes to trial, the accused has the option of selecting a trial by judge or by jury. All these legal steps may take as little time as a week or many months to unfold. At the trial you will have to testify under oath, to identify the accused who will be in the courtroom, and then to recall—to the best of your ability—all circumstances about the crime. You may be questioned by the defense attorney, which should not concern you or make you anxious since you are telling the truth. No matter how many questions you are asked, your answers will always ring true. Thus you should have confidence in yourself and maintain your composure when you are cross-examined. No woman because of fear should hesitate to report a crime and follow the legal procedures outlined here.

Summary

There are three main reasons why it is in your best interest to report every assault, robbery, or threat to your safety. First, the police act only on information supplied by citizens. Without information they have no chance of controlling crime. With proper information they stand the best chance of guaranteeing your safety. The most common complaint we hear from police officers is that people simply don't report crimes that they have witnessed or in which they have been involved. This establishes a vicious circle that renders police ineffective and encourages criminals.

Second, if you fail to report a crime and the police do not apprehend your assailant, there is a possibility that he will attack others or attack you again. If a rapist repeats his crime against you and you then go to the police, it is less likely that you would be believed and that he would be convicted. Thus it is in your own best interest to do everything possible to help apprehend him. To emphasize this point, let us cite the little-known statistic that three-fourths of all serious crimes such as rape, assault, and murder are carried out by persons who do so more than once. This indicates that most criminals repeat their behavior unless arrested. However, once an assailant is arrested, booked, charged, sentenced, and he is subsequently released, it is less likely that he will repeat the crime. He may be deterred by the fact that he has a criminal record and can be easily identified by the police.

Third, we urge you to report every crime to authorities for moral reasons. It is your duty as a responsible citizen to uphold the laws of our society. To report a crime in which you were involved or to which you were witness is as much a responsibility as obeying laws.* If we are to remain a free society, every citizen must cooperate in upholding the laws of our land.

The necessity to report and prosecute every criminal is illustrated by this example. A rape victim in Riverside, California, reported a rapist and began the initial court proceedings. She went as far as the trial and then became intimidated by the questioning to which she was subjected by the defense attorney. Finally, in total frustration, she falsely testified that the man she had accused was not her rapist. This ended the trial and the man was set free—free to rape again, which he did five months later. His second victim was not as fortunate as the first. After raping her he beat her so severely that she died. If the first woman had carried out her obligation to society, the second woman would be alive today.

In the September 24, 1978, issue of *Family Weekly*, William H. Webster, Director of the FBI, was asked "What is the greatest deterrent to crime?" He responded "The greatest deterrent is responsible citizen involvement within the framework of our criminal-justice system by honoring the law yourself and contributing to its honest, impartial enforcement. This means prompt reporting of crimes to which you are a witness or victim. It means willingness to appear in court to offer testimony or to serve on a jury."

*There is a national toll-free number that people can call to report crimes. It is called Eyewitness Anonymous, and the number is (800) 472-7785. If the caller's tip leads to a conviction, a reward is given.

Chapter 10
Shaping Up
for Self-defense

Perhaps we're stretching the term *self-defense* a bit when we include defending yourself against disease and obesity, which are also prevalent culprits in today's society. But no one will debate the importance of daily exercise in our lives. Exercise can be obtained in many different ways. My (Dr. Conroy's) eighty-year-young mother keeps fit through gardening and housekeeping. I am an avid jogger and run between one and a half and three miles a day. You may prefer to bike ride, play tennis, swim, or join a health club. Dr. Ritvo works out in a gym five days a week.

If you have not established a daily pattern of exercise, or you don't have the time or facilities, we recommend that you devote at least fifteen minutes a day to the following exercises. They will be instrumental in firming and toning your entire body. They will also improve your cardiovascular efficiency, strength, flexibility, and endurance, while they prepare your body to practice and execute the physical skills of self-defense. For those of you who do not exercise on a regular basis, we suggest that you perform the minimum number of repetitions in the beginning. Increase the number of exercises on a progressive basis.

As anyone who has had athletic training can tell you, the first days of any conditioning program are the hardest. Muscles and joints protest with stiffness and aching. These discomforts disappear as your body develops increased circulation, improved muscle tone, and joint flexibility. Thus we caution you not to be discouraged at the outset. The price you pay in temporary discomfort will be amply rewarded by dividends of increased self-confidence and physical well-being.

Specific Exercises

Head Rolls

These exercises increase neck strength and suppleness. Stand or sit upright and stretch your neck upward; then drop your chin to your chest. Rotate your neck to the extreme right, backward, left, and forward. After four clockwise rotations, repeat these stretching motions in the opposite direction. (See Figure 10–1.)

FIG. 10-1
HEAD ROLLS

Arm Circles

These exercises increase upper-arm suppleness and shoulder strength. Stand with your feet a few inches apart, and hold your arms straight out to your sides at shoulder level with the elbows stiff and your palms down. Make small circles with your arms and gradually increase the size of the circles. (See Figure 10–2.)

FIG. 10-2
ARM   CIRCLES.

Push-ups

These exercises strengthen your arms, shoulders, neck, and back. Lie face down with the palms of your hands on the floor under your shoulders. Keeping your body straight, push against the floor until your arms are straight. Gently lower your chest back to the floor, and repeat the push-up. (See Figure 10–3.)

FIG. 10-3a, 10-3b PUSH UPS

Straddle Stretches

These exercises increase spine and hip suppleness. Sit on the floor with your legs apart and your knees straight. Grasp your right ankle with the right hand, stretch your left arm overhead, and lower your body side-ways toward your right leg. Hold this position for eight seconds. Repeat this movement to the left side. Then lean forward from your waist and touch your elbows on the floor between your knees. Hold this position also for eight seconds, and then repeat the entire sequence. (See Figure 10 –4.)

FIG. 10-4 STRADDLE STRETCHES

Legs Over

These exercises increase spine and leg suppleness. Lie on your back with both arms at your sides, palms down, and legs together. Draw your knees to your chest, then lift both your legs and body until they are at right angles to the floor. Lower your legs over your head until your toes touch the floor. Next, bring your legs back up to the vertical position, then to the knee-to-chest position, and finish by returning to the starting position. Repeat the entire sequence. (See Figure 10–5.)

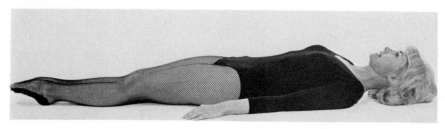

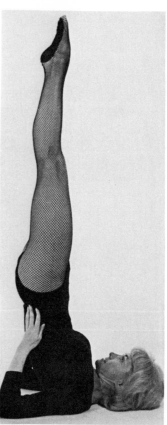

FIG. 10-5   LEGS OVER.

Sit-ups

These exercises strengthen stomach and back muscles. Lie on your back with your arms across your chest and bend your knees. Curl your head and shoulders forward. Return gradually to the lying position. Repeat the sequence. (See Figure 10–6.)

FIG. 10-6   SIT-UPS.

Kneeling Stretches

These exercises stretch the muscles of your upper legs, stomach, chest, and shoulders. Sit in a kneeling position, knees slightly apart, with hands holding your toes. Thrust your hips forward and up so that your back is arched and your arms are extended. Hold for four seconds. Repeat the entire sequence slowly. (See Figure 10–7.)

FIG. 10-7   KNEELING STRETCHES.

Cross-Leg Stretches

These exercises increase spine suppleness and strengthen the muscles of your legs. From a standing position, cross your right leg (knee bent) over your left leg. Lean forward from the hips and try to place your palms on the floor. Hold for eight seconds. Repeat to the opposite side. (See Figure 10–8.)

FIG. 10-8
CROSS-LEG   STRETCHES.

Knee Squats

These exercises strengthen the muscles of your upper legs. Stand with your feet a few inches apart. Lean slightly forward, bend your knees, and squat as far down as you can comfortably go with your heels remaining on the floor. Return to standing position. Repeat this sequence. (See Figure 10–9.)

FIG. 10-9   KNEE SQUATS.

Jump Kicks

These exercises increase leg strength, suppleness, and coordination. They are also excellent for slimming chubby thighs. Stand with feet together, and jump on both feet. Hop on your right foot and kick the left foot forward, keeping the foot flexed. Repeat to the opposite side. Continue rhythmically eight times while increasing the height of the kicks. Repeat this sequence to the side and back. (See Figure 10–10.)

FIG. 10-10 JUMP KICKS.

Leg Raises

These exercises increase flexibility for kicking, and they also tighten the thigh muscles. Lie on one side, raise and lower your top leg rapidly. Repeat the entire sequence while lying on the other side. (See Figure 10–11.)

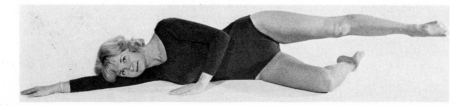

FIG. 10-11 LEG RAISES.

FIG. 10-11 (CONT'D)   LEG RAISES.

Arm Drops

These exercises increase agility and strengthen the muscles of your upper arms. Kneel on a rug or soft surface. Extend your arms in front of your body. Fall forward, allowing your bending arms to absorb the impact of the fall. (See Figure 10–12.)

FIG. 10-12
ARM   DROPS.

Side Bends

These exercises firm and tighten your midriff. Stand with your feet at shoulder-width apart and your right arm above your head. Lean sideward to the left as far as is comfortable. Hold this stance for eight seconds. Repeat this exercise to the right. (See Figure 10–13.)

FIG. 10-13
SIDE BENDS.

Cardiovascular Conditioning

Swimming, jogging, rope jumping, and cycling improve your circulatory system. We highly recommend a daily program of these activities.

Physical Aids to Learning

Although the self-defense tactics we recommend are simple to perform, mastering them takes practice. Because you cannot readily practice gouges, jabs, blows, and kicks on people, we suggest that you use substitute targets. Some of the following "games" will require the aid of a friend to hold the target. You can increase your speed and accuracy if the friend moves the target as you try to hit it. Such game training will perfect your ability to deliver blows without "telegraphing" movements.

Balls

Any type of ball is an excellent target. Remember these points: (1) Do not "telegraph" your blows, (2) aim six to eight inches through the surface you are striking, and (3) stand close enough to hit through it.

1. Have a friend hold a ball securely in both hands in front of his or her body at waist height. Strike the ball as if you are delivering a double-hand blow to the back of the neck.
2. Practice the knee lift to the groin by having a friend hold a ball waist high at his or her side. Strike the ball from the hands with your knee.
3. Practice the thumb gouge to the eyes by having a friend hold a ball to the side of his or her head. Clasp your hands vigorously over the sides of the ball and gouge with your thumbs. (See Figure 10–14.)
4. Practice the finger jab to the eyes on a ball by having a friend hold it to his or her side above the head. Round your fingers slightly and jab the ball from his or her hands.

FIG. 10-14   USING BALL FOR PRACTICING THUMB GOUGE.

Rolled-up Exercise Mats or Sofa Cushions

Rolled-up exercise mats or sofa cushions are excellent targets for practice. Roll the mat tightly and stand it on end.

1. Tape an X on the mat or cushion to identify the knee area. Practice front, side, and rear kicks. (See Figure 10–15.)
2. Put a rolled mat or cushion on a sofa or chair and practice double-hand blows to the top of it.
3. Tilt the mat or cushion forward slightly to practice knee lifts to the groin.
4. Practice a double-knee drop on several stacked cushions or a loosely rolled mat that has been placed on a soft surface.

FIG. 10-15
USING ROLLED MATS FOR PRACTICING KICKS.

Pillows or Rolled Sleeping Bags

You can substitute a pillow or rolled sleeping bag for a ball, cushion, or rolled exercise mat. Have a friend hold a bed pillow or rolled sleeping bag at the appropriate level and call out a man's four vulnerable areas. You can gouge, jab, pull, hit, and kick the pillow with full force and in rapid succession. (See Figures 10-16 through 10-20.)

FIG. 10-16 USING A PILLOW FOR PRACTICING THUMB GOUGE.

FIG. 10-17
FINGER JAB.

FIG. 10-18
GROIN PULL.

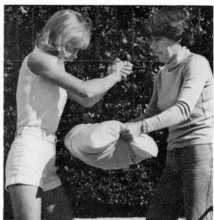

FIG. 10-19   DOUBLE-HAND BLOW.

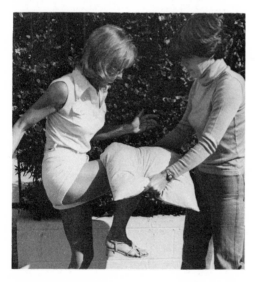

FIG. 10-20
KNEE   IN   GROIN.

Halloween Mask

Enlarge the eyes of a Halloween mask and have a friend hold it up for you to practice finger jabs and thumb gouges.

Golf Balls

This practice technique was created by one of our more imaginative students. Place two golf balls in a stocking tied at the top. Have a friend tuck the top of the stocking into his or her slacks and practice grabbing, squeezing, and then pulling them down and away.

The Numbers Game

Assign a number to each skill. The thumb gouge, which is your best technique, is number 1. The groin pull, which is your second-best technique, is number 2. The finger jab is number 3; the knee in the groin is number 4; the double-hand blow to the back of the neck is number 5; and the kick is number 6. As a friend calls out a number, you perform the correct technique. The numbers should be mixed and called forcefully and rapidly.

Follow-through

Ask a friend to hold a pillow at the appropriate height and call out the four vulnerable areas on the body (eyes, groin, neck, and knee). You then perform the correct skill to the area. Since two techniques are correctly performed to the eyes, your friend should shout "eyes one," to which a thumb gouge will be executed and "eyes two," to which a finger jab will be performed. The same is true of the groin. "Groin one" will indicate a groin pull, "groin two" will indicate a knee into the groin. "Neck" will indicate a double-hand blow; and "knee," a kick. The caller must name the vulnerable areas enthusiastically and rapidly.

With a Little Help from Your Friends

An "Assailant" Partner

A cooperative friend is the best teaching aid you can use. His or her role is to attack you in various ways at unsuspecting moments. Your goal is to escape instantaneously using at least five skills. While your friend is attacking: (1) He or she must be aggressive, and (2) he or she must not release you unless you simulate the correct gouges, jabs, blows, and kicks. Your partner should have a vivid imagination and assume that your simulated kicks and blows are real.

Observe and Describe

Practice identifying and describing people accurately. While with a friend, practice glancing at someone and memorize as much about his or her physical appearance as you can. Close your eyes and describe him or her. Your friend can assess your accuracy of the person's description.

Mental Aids to Learning

Proper mental preparedness is a prerequisite for proper physical preparedness. The following are some ways to increase mental preparedness.

Personal Situations
Write realistic descriptions of how you would defend yourself in the five dangerous situations you listed on page 22.

TV and Movies
When you watch TV programs or attend movies that depict violence, note situations in which the victim neglected to "eliminate," "recognize," and "avoid" danger. Discuss with friends what you would have done in the same situation to eliminate, recognize, and avoid danger and, if it were unavoidable, which tactics you would have used to fight and escape.

Magazines and Newspapers
Save newspaper and magazine articles describing crimes against people and property. Underline descriptions of violence. Then draw up a separate list of the mistakes the victims made. Next to each mistake, write a realistic and effective alternative.

Chapter 11
Twenty Days to a More Powerful and Secure You

Daily Lesson Plans

Activity	Day One	Chapter
Reading:	Introduction to self-defense	1
	Eliminating dangers	2
	Recognizing and avoiding dangers	2
	Talk	
	Run	
	Scream	
	Fighting—but only when necessary	2
	Four vulnerable areas on the man's body	4
	Five best weapons on the woman's body	4
	Legal responsibility for using self-defense	1
Assignment:	List five dangerous situations in which you could find yourself.	2

Day Two

Exercises:	Head rolls (4 times each side)	10
	Arm circles (10 times each direction)	
	Cross-leg stretches (4 times each side)	
	Side bends (4 times each)	
	Straddle stretches (2 times each side)	

Activity   **Chapter**

	Sit-ups (10 times)	
	Arm drops (3 times)	
	Push-ups (3 times)	
Review:	Strategies for self-defense	
	Vulnerable areas and woman's best weapons	
	Legal responsibility for using self-defense	
New Skills:	Talk—"What do you want?"	2
	Relinquish valuables if necessary.	6
	Defensive scream—"Fire, Fire, Fire"	4
	Attacking scream—"Aahhhhhh"	4
	Run.	2

If grabbed—relax body, don't struggle.

Combination 1: You are walking along on a deserted street as an assailant approaches. You change your direction at a 90° angle. Run, scream "fire," drop your purse, and mentally prepare to fight.

Combination 2: You are grabbed from behind in a tight bear hug. Don't struggle, relax your body, and say "What do you want?"

Assignment: Tape a dime (or the price of a phone call) to the inside of your wallet for an emergency phone call.

Day Three

Exercises:	Head rolls (4 times each side)	10
	Side bends (4 times each side)	
	Cross-leg stretches (1 time each side)	
	Push-ups (3 times)	
	Sit-ups (10 times)	
	Kneeling stretch (2 times)	
	Jump kicks (4 times to each side)	
	Legs over (2 times)	
	Leg raises (3 times each side)	
	Sprint 25 yards (2 times).	
Review:	Strategies for self-defense	
	Vulnerable areas on man's body and a woman's best weapons	
	Legal responsibility for using self-defense	
	If grabbed—don't struggle, relax body.	
	Combination 1 (Refer to day 2.)	
	Combination 2 (Refer to day 2.)	
New Skill:	Thumb gouge to the eyes	4

Activity   **Chapter**

(Demonstrate at least five different attack positions in
which the eye gouge could be used successfully.)

Reading: Psychological factors that inhibit aggressive behavior   1

Ingredients of a successful attack: 2

      Speed   Force

      Accuracy   Follow-through

Never fight unless your life or health is in danger.   1

Assignment: Write a list of your valuables.   3

Day Four

Exercises: Head rolls (4 times each side)   10

Side bends (4 times each side)

Cross-leg stretches (1 time each side)

Push-ups (3 times)

Sit-ups (10 times)

Kneeling stretch (2 times)

Jump kicks (4 times to each side)

Legs over (2 times)

Leg raises (8 times each side)

Sprint 25 yards (2 times).

Review: Ingredients for a successful attack

Never fight unless your life or health is in danger.

Combination 1: (Refer to day 2.)

Combination 2: (Refer to day 2.)

New Skill: Groin pull: Use two golf balls tied in a long stocking.   4

(Demonstrate five different attack positions in which
the groin pull could be used successfully.)

Combination 3: A man grabs your throat from the
front with both of his hands. Scream as you deliver a
thumb gouge, a groin pull, and run screaming "fire,
fire."

Combination 4: A man grabs you from behind in a
tight bear hug and is about to throw you over a cliff.
Since you must react immediately, scream as you deliver a groin pull, turn and execute a thumb gouge, and
run screaming "fire, fire."

Reading: Fear and panic (If you panic, do nothing physical. Wait   2
until you can react properly.)

Assignment: Make two lists of emergency phone numbers. Tape one   3
to your telephone, and place the other in your wallet.

Activity   **Chapter**

Day Five

Exercises:	Head rolls (4 times each side)	10
	Arm circles (10 times each direction)	
	Knee squats (4 times)	
	Kneeling stretches (2 times)	
	Push-ups (4 times)	
	Sit-ups (14 times)	
	Straddle stretches (2 times each side)	
	Jump kicks (4 times each side)	
	Sprint 25 yards (2 times).	
Review:	Groin pull	
	Combinations 3 and 4 (Refer to day 4.)	
	Fear and panic	
New Skills:	Finger jab (Demonstrate five different attack positions from which the finger jab could be used successfully.)	4
	Play the numbers game one through three.	10
	Dating dangers	6
Assignment:	List ten rules of personal safety that you should follow at home, work, school, and in public areas.	3

Day Six

Reading:	The golden rules of personal safety	3
	Eliminating danger: State, in five words or less, five ways to eliminate danger.	2
	Recognizing and avoiding danger:	2
	Describe five potentially dangerous situations and suggest ways to avoid them.	

Day Seven

Exercises:	Head rolls (4 times each side)	10
	Arm circles (10 times each direction)	
	Side bends (4 times each side)	
	Knee squats (5 times)	
	Sit-ups (16 times)	
	Push-ups (4 times)	
	Kneeling stretches (3 times)	
	Jump kicks (8 times each side)	
	Sprint 25 yards (2 times).	
Review:	Finger jab	
	Combinations 3 and 4 (Refer to day 4.)	

Activity   **Chapter**

New Skills: Knee blow to the groin   4
            Double-hand blow to the back of the neck   4
            Combination 5: A man standing directly in front of
            you grabs both of your wrists. Scream as you deliver a
            knee to the groin, a double-hand blow to the back of his
            neck, and run screaming "fire, fire."
            Play the numbers game one through five.   10
            Combination 6: A man wearing tight jeans has grabbed
            one arm and is pulling you toward his car. Scream as
            you deliver a finger jab to the eyes, a knee blow to the
            groin, and run screaming "fire, fire."
Reading: Dealing with an exhibitionist   3
            Mental preparedness—the key to self-defense   1

Day Eight

Exercises: Arm circles (10 times each direction)   10
            Straddle stretches (2 times each side)
            Arm drops (3 times)
            Cross-leg stretches (4 times each side)
            Legs over (2 times)
            Push-ups (4 times)
            Sit-ups (16 times)
            Sprint 25 yards (2 times).
Review: Knee blow to the groin
            Double-hand blow to the back of the neck
            Combinations 5 and 6 (Refer to day 7.)
New Skills: Kicks—front, side, and rear   4
            (Kick into cushions or rolled sleeping bags.)
            Play the numbers game one through six.   10
            Combination 7: A man, wearing tight jeans, grabs your
            throat from behind with both of his hands. Scream as
            you deliver a rear kick, turn and execute a thumb gouge
            to the eyes, a double-hand blow to the back of his neck,
            and run screaming "fire, fire."
            Combination 8: A very tall man, wearing tight jeans, is
            strangling you from the front with both of his hands on
            your throat. His arms are fairly straight and his head is
            back, thus making a thumb gouge difficult. Scream as
            you deliver a front kick to his knee, and as he releases
            your throat, execute a thumb gouge to his eyes. Follow
            through with a double-hand blow to the back of his

Activity   **Chapter**

	neck and run screaming "fire, fire."	
Reading:	Dangers from vicious dogs	6

Day Nine

Exercises:	Head rolls (2 times each side)	10
	Kneeling stretches (3 times)	
	Straddle stretches (2 times each side)	
	Knee squats (6 times)	
	Leg raises (8 times each side)	
	Push-ups (5 times)	
	Sit-ups (10 times)	
	Arm drops (3 times)	
	Sprint 25 yards (2 times).	
Review:	Kicks	
	Play the numbers game one through six.	10
New Skills:	Ground kicks—kicking an assailant who is on the	4
	ground	
	Review combinations 3 and 4 (refer to day 4). Then follow through with ground kicks to the head and neck and run screaming "fire, fire."	
	Review combinations 5 and 6 (refer to day 7). Follow through with ground kicks to the head and neck, and then run screaming "fire, fire."	
Reading:	When dealing with a robber or a burglar, always give up your valuables.	6

Day Ten

Exercises:	Arm circles (10 times each direction)	10
	Cross-leg stretches (4 times each side)	
	Side bends (4 times each side)	
	Push-ups (5 times)	
	Sit-ups (18 times)	
	Jump kicks (8 times each side)	
	Arm drops (3 times)	
	Sprint 25 yards (2 times).	
Review:	Ground kicks	
	Combinations 3 through 6 (refer to days 4 and 7). Follow through with ground kicks.	
New Skills:	Knee breaks	4
	Double-knee drop	4

Activity   **Chapter**

Combinations 3 through 6 (refer to days 4 and 7). Follow through with ground kicks and, once the assailant is unconscious, knee breaks and/or a double-knee drop.

Reading: Defenses against children   6
             Defenses against women   6
Assignment: Contact your local police department or library and   3
             borrow their electronic marking pencil. Engrave your social security number on all valuables. Place warning tags stating: "All items of value on these premises have been marked for ready identification by Law Enforcement Agencies" on doors and windows.

Day Eleven

Exercises: Arm circles (10 times each direction)   10
             Side bends (4 times each side)
             Legs over (2 times)
             Jump kicks (8 times each side)
             Arm drops (3 times)
             Leg raises (8 times each side)
             Sit-ups (16 times)
             Push-ups (4 times)
             Sprint 25 yards (2 times).
Review: Knee breaks
             Double-knee drop
             Play the numbers game one through six.   10
New Skills: Game—follow through   10
             Suffocation defense   4
             Combination 9: An assailant is suffocating you in bed with a pillow over your face. Execute a thumb gouge, a groin pull, leap to your feet, and follow through with kicks. Run screaming "fire, fire."
             Strangulation defense
             Combination 10: An assailant strangles you from the rear with an article such as a pillowcase. Turn, scream, and execute a thumb gouge to his eyes, a knee to his groin, a double-hand blow to the back of his neck, follow through with ground kicks to his head and neck, and run screaming "fire, fire."
Reading: Forceful intruder   6

Day Twelve

Exercises: Straddle stretches (2 times each side)   10
               Legs over (2 times)
               Kneeling stretches (3 times)
               Cross-leg stretches (4 times each side)
               Leg raises (8 times each side)
               Arm drop (3 times)
               Push-ups (5 times)
               Sit-ups (20 times)
               Sprint 25 yards (2 times).
Review: Strangulation with a rope or tie
New Skills: Defense against weapons—guns, knives, bludgeons   5
               Combination 11: A knife-wielding assailant has cor-
               nered you. Scream as you thrust your hand across your
               body; grasp his wrist firmly and force the knife aside.
               Deliver a finger jab to his eyes with your free hand.
               Run screaming "fire, fire."
               Combination 12: A gun-wielding assailant is holding
               you at bay. As you offer him your valuables, slowly
               move toward him. Once you are very close, scream as
               you thrust your arm across your body, grasp the gun
               barrel and force it away from your body. Simultane-
               ously deliver a finger jab into his eyes. Immediately get
               behind the assassin and hurry silently toward safety.
               Combination 13: An assailant, wielding a tire iron at-
               tempts to strike you. Scream as you leap toward him,
               and simultaneously execute a thumb gouge to his eyes.
               Follow through with a double-hand blow to the back of
               his neck, kicks, and run screaming "fire, fire."
Reading: Murder   6

Day Thirteen

Exercises: Head roll (4 times each side)   10
               Arm circles (10 times each direction)
               Push-ups (5 times)
               Sit-ups (20 times)
               Side bends (4 times each side)
               Leg over (2 times)
               Jump kicks (8 times each side)
               Cross-leg stretches (4 times each side)
               Knee squats (8 times)

Activity   **Chapter**

Sprint 25 yards (2 times).
Review: Combinations 11 through 13 (Refer to day 12.)
Play the numbers game one through six.   10
New Skills: Ground maneuvers   4
Combination 14: A man has thrown you to the ground
and is sitting on top of you, holding one wrist, and tear-
ing at your clothing. Execute a finger jab, roll him off
you, leap to your feet, and follow through with kicks.
Run screaming "fire, fire."
Combination 15: You awaken from a deep sleep to find
a man lying on top of you, strangling you with both
hands. Execute a thumb gouge, and with your thumbs
in his eyes roll him off screaming "fire, fire."
Reading: Rape (myths, rape crisis center, when to submit, how to   8
convince assailant not to rape you)

Day Fourteen

Exercises: Head rolls (4 times each side)   10
Arm circles (10 times each direction)
Knee squats (6 times)
Kneeling stretch (3 times)
Push-ups (2 times)
Sit-ups (22 times)
Jump kicks (8 times each side)
Sprint 25 yards (2 times).
Review: Rape
Ground maneuvers
Combinations 14 and 15 (Refer to day 13.)
New Skill: Hair maneuvers   4
Combination 16: An assailant grabs your hair and at-
tempts to pull you into the bushes. Execute a hair ma-
neuver and follow through with kicks. Run screaming
"fire, fire."
Reading: Misuse of weapons (hair sprays, chemical tear gas, nail   5
files, purse items, whistles, pepper, hat pins, broken
bottles, knives, guns)

Day Fifteen

Exercises: Head rolls (4 times each side)   10
Side bends (4 times each side)

Activity   **Chapter**

	Kneeling stretch (3 times)	
	Sit-ups (24 times)	
	Push-ups (6 times)	
	Jump kicks (8 times)	
	Leg raises (8 times each side)	
	Arm drop (3 times)	
	Sprint 25 yards (2 times).	
Review:	Hair maneuvers	
	Combination 16 (Refer to day 14.)	
	Play the numbers game one through six.	10
New Skill:	Defense against women	6
Reading:	Attacks on children	7
	Attacks by children	6
	Child abuse	7

Day Sixteen

Exercises:	Arm circles (10 times each direction)	10
	Cross-leg stretches (4 times each side)	
	Side bends (4 times each side)	
	Push-ups (7 times)	
	Sit-ups (24 times)	
	Kneeling stretches (3 times)	
	Jump kicks (8 times each side)	
	Sprint 25 yards (2 times).	
Review:	Defense against women	
	Combinations 14 through 16 (Refer to days 13 and 14.)	
	Play the numbers game one through six.	10
	Play the follow-through game using the pillow.	
New Skill:	Defense against two or more assailants	6
Reading:	Identifying criminals	9
	Reporting assaults to the police	9
	The criminal trial	9

Day Seventeen

Review entire book for your written examination.

Day Eighteen

Exercises:	Head rolls (4 times each side)	10
	Arm circles (10 times each direction)	

Side bends (4 times each side)
Sit-ups (25 times)
Push-ups (8 times)
Jump kicks (8 times each side)
Straddle stretches (2 times each side)
Legs over (2 times)
Sprint 25 yards (2 times).

Review: Thumb gouge, groin pull, finger jab, knee blow to the groin, double-hand blow, kicks, knee break and double-knee drop using cushions, pillows and/or rolled sleeping bags.

Reading: Woman beating   6
Threat of being bound   6
Bunco   6

Day Nineteen

Written
Examin-
ation: Complete the 35-question, true/false, multiple-choice,   11
fill-in examination in this book. Each correct answer receives 1 point, to equal a total of 35 points for the written examination.

Answer key:

1. F	13. F	25. b, c, d, e
2. T	14. F	26. c
3. T	15. F	27. a, b, c, d, e
4. T	16. T	28. e
5. T	17. c	29. c, e
6. T	18. a, b, d, e	30. d
7. F	19. a, b, c, d, e	31. dead bolt
8. F	20. a, b, c, d	32. a. knee
9. F	21. a, c, d, e	b. groin
10. F	22. c	c. throat
11. F	23. c	d. eyes
12. F	24. b, c, d, e	33. a. voice
		b. fingers and thumbs
		c. hands
		d. legs
		e. knee
		34. a. speed

Activity   **Chapter**

        b. power
        c. accuracy
        d. follow-through
     35. a. eliminate danger
        b. recognize and avoid danger
        c. fight

Assignment: Describe in writing the strategies and tactics you should employ to escape from the five dangerous situations that you listed in lesson 1. (Allocate 1 point per correct situation, for a total of 5 points.)

Day Twenty

Exercises: Arm circles (10 times each direction)   10
                Leg raises (8 times each side)
                Cross-leg stretch (4 times each side)
                Side bends (4 times)
                Sit-ups (25 times)
                Push-ups (6 times)
                Jump kicks (8 times each side)
                Arm drops (3 times)
                Kneeling stretch (3 times)
                Sprint 25 yards (2 times).
Review: All skills using cushions, pillows, and rolled sleeping bags
                Combinations 1 through 16 (Refer to days 2 through 14.)

Your Final Practical Examination

Exercises: Head rolls (4 times each side)   10
                Cross-leg stretch (8 times each side)
                Sit-ups (25 times)
                Leg over (2 times)
                Push-ups (6 times)
                Jump Kicks (8 times each side)
                Knee squats (8 times)
                Leg raises (8 times each side)
                Sprint 25 yards (2 times).

Skills	Number of points per skill	Number of points per section
Combination kicks: front/side or rear/side. (Kick into cushions or rolled sleeping bags.)	5	25
Combination moves: rear kick, turn, double-hand blow to the back of the neck. (Kick, turn, and hit the top of the cushion or rolled sleeping bag.)	5	
Thumb gouge (Use a pillow); knee blow into the groin; double-hand blow to the back of the neck (use cushions).	5	
Finger jab (use a pillow); groin pull (use two golf balls in a stocking); side kick (use cushions or rolled sleeping bag).	5	
Screams	5	

Defense in a dangerous situation:	5	10

Select two—forceful intruder, overzealous date, vicious dog, exhibitionist, gang of children, child beating, violent women, robber, two or more assailants, bunco, woman beating, threat of being bound, rapist, murderer.

Defense against a weapon: Select one— gun, knife, bludgeon.	5	10
Combination blows: Have a friend hold a pillow at each appropriate level and call out the four vulnerable areas, as you strike the areas in rapid succession using the correct blows.	5	
Attacks: Have a friend attack you three times. You will not be told how you will be grabbed. Suggested attacks are the front, side, or rear bear hug; front, side, or rear choke; hair; single-wrist or double-wrist grasp; strangulation; suffocation with a pillow; ground and unconventional. You must perform at least five skills and run fifteen steps screaming "fire, fire."	5 points each	15
	Total	60

Scoring Yourself   **Points**

Total Written examination........................ 35

Description of your five dangerous situ-
ations...5

Total practical examination....................... 60

                                                  100   total points

TEST YOUR KNOWLEDGE

(Answers are listed in Chapter 11, Day 19.)

True or False

If the statement is true, write T. If the statement is false, write F.

1. _____An alert woman who has eliminated, recognized, and avoided every potential danger she can imagine is safe.

2. _____A good rule of self-defense is: "Whenever possible, run or talk—don't fight."

3. _____Most "self-defense" requires no physical skill.

4. _____Blows and kicks should *always* be aimed through your target, not at it.

5. _____A man who commits rape has most likely committed similar offenses in the past.

6. _____Violence rather than sexual pleasure is the major concern of many rapists.

7. _____The groin is the most vulnerable area on a man's body.

8. _____To avoid locking yourself out of your home, it is wise to hide a key in your mailbox or under your doormat.

9. _____You are riding alone on a bus. A man continues to bother you. Your best tactic is to avoid trouble by getting off at the next stop.

10. _____Screaming "help" is wiser than screaming "fire" if there are other people around who may assist you.

11. _____If possible, it is safest and most humane to hurt an assailant rather than injure him.

12. _____Your defensive tactics are exactly the same against male and female assailants.

13. _____You return home to find your front door ajar. Your best tactic is: Do not enter your home alone. Ask a strong burly neighbor to enter with you.

14. _____It is safe to hitchhike with two burly male friends because if trouble arises they can protect you.
15. _____While walking alone on the beach, you are approached by a man. He harasses you, pinches your bottom, and makes lewd remarks. Your best strategy is to tell him you know self-defense. If he continues to bother you, scream, dislocate his knee, and run.
16. _____Never fight unless your life or health is in danger, because your physical defense may not be successful.

Multiple Choice

Choose the correct *answer* or *answers*. If any portion of your answer is incorrect, do not give yourself credit for the question. Please read *each possibility* carefully.

17. The safest way to list yourself (as a single woman) in the telephone directory is by
   a. last name only.
   b. first and last name.
   c. initials of first and middle names plus last name.
   d. first name only.
   e. middle name plus last name.
18. If you must submit to rape, you should
   a. remain calm.
   b. obtain a clear description of the assailant.
   c. shower and douche.
   d. notify the police.
   e. have a medical examination.
19. Purse weapons can be more of a hindrance than help because
   a. time can be wasted by hunting for them.
   b. they can be taken away from you.
   c. they can be used against you.
   d. aiming an object is more difficult than aiming your hand.
   e. your confidence is in the object rather than in yourself.
20. The best tactic(s) for eliminating obscene phone calls is (are) to
   a. hang up.
   b. blow a whistle into the mouthpiece.
   c. tap a pencil on the mouthpiece and say, "Officer, this is the obscene phone call I told you about and now you can trace the line."
   d. have an unlisted phone number.
   e. ask the caller for his name and address and report him to the police.
21. When reporting any emergency by telephone to the operator or police state
   a. your name.

    b. your age.

    c. the phone number from which you are calling.

    d. the address where the emergency is taking place.

    e. the nature of the emergency.

22. You are attending a movie unescorted. The man sitting next to you places his hand on your knee. You should

    a. scream "fire" to frighten him off and alert those around you to your problem.

    b. execute a finger pull to let him know you mean business.

    c. move.

    d. place your hand on his thigh.

    e. threaten him with the fact that you know self-defense.

23. Your neighbors are away for a two-week vacation. On the eighth day, a moving van pulls into their driveway and begins loading their furniture. Your best tactic(s) is (are) to

    a. ask the men moving the furniture for proper identification.

    b. get your husband or boyfriend to request identification.

    c. notify the police.

    d. ignore the situation because it is none of your business.

    e. tell the men they are thieves and threaten to call the police.

24. A man on the street *continues* to follow you. Your best tactic(s) is (are) to

    a. avoid eye contact to prevent his knowing you are suspicious of him.

    b. run.

    c. scream "fire, fire."

    d. drop your purse.

    e. mentally prepare for a counterattack.

25. Whenever possible, it is best to

    a. use the finger jab rather than the thumb gouge.

    b. use the groin pull rather than the finger jab.

    c. scream "fire" rather than "help."

    d. talk rather than fight.

    e. describe to the police the assailant's physical characteristics rather than his attire.

26. You are walking in a park when you see a woman thirty yards away under attack by a knife-wielding man. You should

    a. run to the woman's aid by attacking the man with screams, kicks, and blows.

    b. watch the entire attack so that you can appear in court as her witness.

    c. leave the poor woman with the assailant and call the police.

    d. ignore the attack because "self-defense" indicates that you are trained to take care of yourself.

e. tell a burly passerby to try to stop the fight physically.

27. You are home alone when the doorbell rings. You look through the safety viewer and see an unsolicited man in a telephone repair uniform. You should
    a. have a conversation with an imaginary friend.
    b. ask the man what he wants.
    c. check the man's identification card.
    d. call the telephone company if you are suspicious.
    e. notify the police if the man is a fraud.

28. Along with learning skills in self-defense, your book recommends that you become proficient in
    a. the use of small handguns.
    b. throwing objects, such as lamps and rolling pins, accurately.
    c. karate, judo, or other martial arts.
    d. the use of purse weapons, such as hair spray and a nail file.
    e. none of these.

29. A man grabs your throat with both of his hands in a front choke. You should
    a. grasp his little fingers with both hands to release the choke. Follow through with a kick to his knee, a double-hand blow to the back of his neck, ground kicks, and run screaming "fire, fire."
    b. do nothing because you could make him angry.
    c. scream as you deliver a thumb gouge to his eyes, a knee in his groin, a double-hand blow to the back of his neck, follow through with kicks, and run screaming "fire, fire."
    d. thrust both of your arms up between his arms to release the choke, follow through with a thumb gouge, groin pull, ground kicks, and run screaming "fire, fire."
    e. report the attack to the police.

30. A friend of yours "flips out" and attempts to hit you. You should
    a. kick toward his knee to let him know you mean business.
    b. hit him (but not really hard) to let him know you mean business.
    c. defend yourself by delivering powerful kicks and blows.
    d. run away.
    e. tell him you know self-defense and will use it on him.

Fill in the Blanks

Write your answers clearly. If any part of the answer is incorrect, no credit will be given.

31. The safest lock you can purchase is a _____

32. List the four *most* vulnerable areas of a man's body.
    a. _____
    b. _____
    c. _____
    d. _____

33. List the five *best* bodily weapons on a woman.
    a. _____
    b. _____
    c. _____
    d. _____
    e. _____

34. List (according to your book) the four necessary ingredients for a successful attack.
    a. _____
    b. _____
    c. _____
    d. _____

35. List the three strategies of self-defense.
    a. _____
    b. _____
    c. _____

Self-defense Resource List

Books
  Amier, Menachem. *Patterns in Forcible Rape.* Chicago: University of
    Chicago Press, 1971.
  Berns, Walter. *For Capital Punishment.* New York: Basic Books, 1979.
  Brownmiller, Susan. *Against Our Will: Men, Women and Rape.* New
    York: Simon and Schuster, 1975.
  Conroy, Mary, and Edward R. Ritvo. *Common Sense Self Defense.* St.
    Louis, Mo.: Mosby Publishing Company, 1977.
  Crime in the United States. Uniform Crime Reports, Federal Bureau of
    Investigation, U.S. Department of Justice. Washington, D.C.: U.S.
    Government Printing Office, 20402, 1979.
  Csida, June Bundy, and Joseph Csida. *Rape—How to Avoid It and
    What to Do About It If You Can't.* Chatsworth, Calif.: Books for
    Better Living, 1974.
  Medea, Andra, and Kathleen Thompson. *Against Rape.* New York:
    Farrar, Strauss and Giroux, 1974.
  Queen's Bench Foundation. *Rape: Prevention and Resistance.* San
    Francisco, Calif., 1976.
Film
  Common Sense Self-Defense. Mary Conroy, Department of Physical
    Education, California State University, Los Angeles. 5151 State
    University Drive, Los Angeles, California 90032.
    Price: $500.00, Rental $75.00.
National Organizations
  Commission on the Status of Women. National Organization for
    Women (NOW), Rape Crisis Center, local and state chapters.
  Rape Crisis Center Newsletter, P.O. Box 21005, Washington, D.C.,
    20009.

About the Authors

Mary Conroy, Ed.D., is one of the nation's leading authorities on self-defense. She received a doctorate degree in education from Columbia University, New York, and is now a professor of physical education at California State University, Los Angeles. While in graduate school, she was accosted at knifepoint by a robber. She managed to do all the wrong things, and the police reprimanded her for her carelessness. She decided to study self-defense and has been teaching, studying and researching it ever since—nearly eighteen years. All her instructors have been men—experts in karate, judo, kung fu, or police science. She took their most effective techniques, rejected those that work for men but not women, and added some tricky fighting and common sense to formulate the program on self-defense for women she gives in this book.

Dr. Conroy's unique program of self-defense has been adopted in high schools, colleges and universities throughout the United States. Her self-defense series, broadcast on educational television, is being used by the California State Board of Education to train teachers and students in their 1,300 school districts.

Mary has received particular recognition for conducting clinics to train police officers, teachers, students, and citizens in her methods of self-defense. She also serves as consultant to the Commission on the Status of Women and to the Los Angeles and San Francisco Police Departments. Her lectureships have taken her to school, community, and corporate organizations throughout North America. She is a familiar personality on television talk shows, including "The John Davidson Show," "Hour Magazine," "The Mike Douglas Show," and "Good Morning America." A public-broadcasting-system television series by Dr. Conroy entitled "Emergency Minutes" received an Emmy Award nomination. She also produced and appeared in an award-winning educational film entitled *Common Sense Self-Defense*, which has been widely distributed throughout the United States and other countries. At five feet four inches tall and weighing 105 pounds she demonstrates that every woman can learn to protect herself.

Edward R. Ritvo, M.D., graduated from Harvard College in 1951 and Boston University School of Medicine in 1955. He is a diplomate of the American Board of Psychiatry and Neurology in Adult and Child Psychiatry and has served as a consultant to court clinics and juvenile authorities in Massachusetts, Texas, and California. Presently he is a professor in the division of child psychiatry and mental retardation at the UCLA School of Medicine.

INDEX

A

Accuracy in delivery, 20
Aching (and exercise), 155
Alertness, 2, 8, 10, 45, 93
Aggravated assault, 3, 110-111
  and fighting, 111
Arm circles, 157
Arm drop, 165
Arms, exercises for, 158, 165
Artist's composite sketch, 151
Assailant(s)
  blinding of, 18
  describing, 149-50
  incapacitating, 18-20, 45
  insufficiently incapacitating,
    64
  killing, 86
    legal justification for, 86
  picking out of lineup, 152
  sued by, 7
  and trial, 152
  two or more, 109-110
  See also Self-defense and
    Tactics
Assertiveness, 10-11
Anxiety, 4, 10, 11
  while learning self-defense,
    4-5
Atlanta Youth Murderer, 119

B

Baby-sitter, precautions with, 29
Back muscles, exercise for, 161
Balls (as practice targets), 167
Bianchi, Kenneth (Hillside
  Strangler), 116
Bludgeon attack, defense
  against, 49, 91
  and not blocking, 91
Book (as weapon), 81
Bound by assailant, 106
  danger of, 106
Break-ins, discouraging, 29-30

  See also Burglars, Burglary
Broom (as weapon), 83
Brownmiller, Susan, 128
Bunco crimes, 93-95
  embarrassment and, 95
  Gypsy scam as, 94
  preventing, 94-95
Burglars, ploys of, 26, 103, 104
Burglary, 102-106
  discouraging, 29-30
    with lights, 29
    with radio, 29
  examples of, 12, 29, 30, 103,
    104
  how to react during, 105-106
  precautions, 29-30
  statistics, 1, 2, 102

C

Capote, Truman, 106
Car
  and hitchhikers, 35
  locking doors of, 35
  precautions, 34-35
  stranded in, 36
  valuables in, 35
Cardiovascular efficiency, 155
  exercise for, 166
Carver, Carolyn, 144
Cash (in house), 28
Chest, exercise for, 162
Child molestation, 119-25
  and fighting, 123
  and guilt, 125
  incest as, 120
  minimizing psychological
    damage, 125
  protecting children from,
    119-25
  reporting, 121, 125
Child molesters
  fantasies of, 120

psychiatric studies of, 119
Clothes, appropriate, 96
Conditioning program, 155-67
Conroy Method of Self-defense,
    3, 46, 47-76, 79, 100, 107,
    111
  against murderers, 111
  against rape, 147
  Seven Tactics of, 46-76
  See also Self-defense and
    Tactics
Counterattack, 6, 8, 47, 65
  See also Conroy Method, Self-
    defense, and Tactics
Crime statistics, 1, 2
  aggravated assault, 1, 2, 110-
    111
  burglary, 1, 2, 102
  murder, 1, 2, 111
  rape, 1, 2, 127, 137
  robbery, 1, 2, 107
Cross-leg stretches, 162
Cycling, 166

D

Dangerous situations
  alertness and, 2, 11, 93
  avoiding, 2, 11-13
  eliminating, 2, 11
  examples of, 1, 2, 5, 6, 8,
    11-12, 20-21, 46, 49, 78,
    93-117, 131, 133, 134, 135,
    136, 139
  fighting in, 2, 6, 16, 18, 86-91,
    101, 111-17, 135, 136, 137-
    38, 147
    See also Self-defense and
      Tactics
  life-threatening, 86-91, 111-17
  panic in, 11
  recognizing, 11-13
  weapons (assailant's), 86-91

when to fight, 2, 6, 16, 18, 86-
    91, 101, 111-17, 135,
    137-38, 147
Dating
  dangers, 95-97
  rules for, 96
Dates, overzealous, 96-97
  psychology of, 97
De Salvo, Albert (Boston Stran-
    gler), 114
Delivery (in self-defense), 20-21
  telegraphing, 167
  See also Self-defense and
    Tactics
Deliverymen, precautions with,
    26
Denial, 10, 11
  and rape, 112
Denver Anti-Crime Council,
    137
Door
  locks on, 24-25
  viewer, 26
Double-hand blow, 17, 47, 59,
    66, 137, 171
  delivery, 59
  practicing, 171
  and speed, 59
  when to use, 59
Double-knee Drop, 74-75, 76
Double-wrist maneuver, 66-67
Drug addicts and crime, 86, 107

E

Elevators, precautions in, 34
Endurance, 155
Eyes (as target area), 18, 47, 56
  See also Finger jab and Thumb
    gouge
Exercise
  frequency of, 155
  program for self-defense,
    155-72

Exhibitionists, 41-42
  avoiding, 42

F

FBI Uniform Crime Report, 1,
  110, 111, 127
"Fightback" (television program), 77
Fighting
  Conroy Method, 3, 46, 47-76,
  79
  immobilizing assailant, 18,
  45, 64
  planning counterattack, 16-17
  tactics to avoid, 14-16
  target areas, 18-20
  techniques
  See Tactics
  when necessary, 2, 6, 16, 18,
  86-91, 101, 111-17, 135,
  137-38, 147
  when stabbed, 111
  See also Self-defense and
  Tactics
Finger jab, 47, 56-57, 71, 72, 87,
  112
  against assailant with gun, 89
  and blindness, 56
  eyes and, 56
  four-finger, 56
  with glasses, 56
  practicing, 167, 169, 171
  when stabbed, 87
Fingers and thumbs (as
  weapons), 16, 48-53,
  56-57, 77, 92
  See also Finger jab and Thumb
  gouge
Five dangerous situations, 9
  list for, 22
Flashlight (as weapon), 82
Flexibility, 155
Front choke maneuver, 68

bent arm, 68
  straight arm, 69
Follow-through, 20
Force, sufficient, 7, 20
Forceful intruder, 105-106
  counterattacking immediately, 105

G

Gangs, 98, 101, 109-110
Genovese, Kitty, 113
Groin (as target area), 18, 47,
  53-55
  See also Groin pull
Groin pull, 17, 47, 53-55, 66, 69,
  71, 72, 136, 138
  delaying, 55, 63
  effectiveness of, 53, 55
  pain and, 54
  practicing, 55, 169, 170, 171
  and rape, 54-55, 136, 138
  starting position, 53
  and tight pants, 54-55
Ground maneuver, 72-75
  lying position, 72
  sitting position, 72
Gun
  defense against, 89-96
  grabbing, 89, 147
  waiting for assailant to put
  down, 89

H

Hair maneuver, 71-72
Hands (as weapons), 16, 77, 92
  See also Finger jab, Groin pull,
  Thumb gouge
Head rolls, 156
Hearst, Patricia, 27
Hillside Strangler, 80, 116
Hitchhiking, 35
  and rape, 35
Home
  precautions in, 23-34

safety devices in, 23-27
Horowitz, David, 77
Howenstein, Sheriff Al, 147
How not to meet men, 95

I
Incest, 120, 123
  hidden, 123
  statistics, 123
  as unspoken crime, 123
In Cold Blood, 106
Intruders
  use of force with, 105
  when to attack, 105

J
Jogging, 166
Jump kicks, 164

K
Kemper, Edward Emil III, 115
Keys 27, 28
  as weapons, 82
Kick(s), 8, 17, 47, 59-64
  aiming, 61, 63
  difficulty of, 17
  difficulty of blocking, 59
  front, 61-62
  heel and instep, 61
  incorrect, 60
  power of, 59
  practicing, 61, 67, 171
  rear, 62-64, 69
  shoes and, 59
  side, 62-63
  target of, 61
  telegraphing, 61
  three-step, 64
Killing assailant in self-defense,
  86
  legality of, 86
Knee (as targets), 19, 57, 64
  breaking, 64
  dislocating, 19

Knee (as weapon), 17, 47, 77
Knee blow, 47, 57-58, 66
  difficulty of, 57
Knee break, 64
Knee lift, 57
  as secondary attack, 57
Knee squats, 163
Kneeling stretches, 162
Knife attack
  blocking, 87
  defense against, 86-88

L
Legal definition of self-defense,
  7
Leg raises, 164
Legs
  exercises for, 160, 162, 163,
    164
  as strongest part of body, 59
  as weapons, 17, 59, 77, 92
Legs over, 160
Life-threatening situations,
  86-91, 111-17
  See also Dangerous situations
Lights, turned on in home, 29
Lock(s)
  chain, 25
  door, 24-25
  poor, 24
  proper, 24
  types of, 24
  window, 25, 26
Los Angeles County Commission on Assaults Against
  Women, 78
Los Angeles Freeway Killer,
  119-20
Los Angeles Police Department,
  20, 29, 55

M
Mace, 77
Magazine (as weapon), 82

Male chauvinism, 79
  and rape, 129
Maneuvers, 65-74
  unconventional, 72
Materials for exercise and practice, 167-72
Mats, 168
Meir, Golda, 130
Men, vulnerable areas on, 18-20
Mental habits, bad, 10
Midriff, exercise for, 166
MIT, 111
Mop handle (as weapon), 83
Mug shots, 151
Murder, 111-17
  Conroy Method and, 111
  self-defense against, 111-12
  statistics, 1, 2, 111
Muscle tone, 155

N

National Neighborhood Watch Program, 32
National Science Foundation, 111
Neck (as target), 20, 47
Neck strength, 156
  exercises for, 158
Newspaper (as weapon), 82
Noisemakers, 80

O

O'Donnell, Lynn, 147

P

Package (as weapon), 81
Panic in dangerous situations, 11
Pen (as weapon), 84
Pelvic examination (after rape), 141
Personal safety, rules for, 23-42
Physical attack (against assailant)
  appropriate force, 7, 45
  delivery, 20-21, 167
  immobilizing assailant, 18, 45
  planning, 16-17
  practicing, 45, 167-72
  tactics for, 45-76
  targeting, 18-20
  See also Self-defense and Tactics
Pickett, Judge Walter, 130
Pickpocket, 42
Pillows (for practice),168
Police, 20-21, 30-31, 65, 95, 105, 107, 125, 135, 140, 149-53
  cooperating with, 31, 149-52
Postrape action, 140-43
Practice and exercise plan (twenty-day), 173-85
Practice of skills, 168-72
  necessity of, 167
  with partner, 171
Proxmire, William, 89
Psychological resistance to learning self-defense, 2
Psychosis and crime, 86, 132
Public transportation and assailants, 37
Purse (as weapon), 77, 78
Purse contents (as weapon), 85
Purse snatching, 42
Push-ups, 158

R

Rape, 3, 4, 5, 11, 13, 35, 37, 46, 49, 89, 109, 112-17, 127-47
  alcohol and, 132
  analysis of cases, 139, 145-46, 147
  anger and, 143
  anxiety and, 142
  attitudes toward, 129-31
  Conroy Method and, 147
  defense against, 54-55, 114,

127-47
See also Tactics
definitions of, 127
denial in, 112
dropping charges, 153
drugs and, 132
emotionally charged nature
   of, 129
examples of, 134, 135, 136,
   139, 145
fighting, 5, 46, 113, 114, 131,
   135, 136, 137-38, 147
fleeing, 135
guilt and, 142
and gun, 89, 147
historical background of, 129
and hitchhiking, 35
and knife, 87
legal action and, 142
and male chauvinism, 129
medical examination, 141
misconceptions concerning,
   129-31
murder, 112-17
   and fighting, 113, 114
   prevention of, 113
panic and, 142
and postrape action, 140-43
pretending to surrender, 142
psychological reaction to, 142
psychology of assailant, 131-
   32
psychosis and, 132
repelling, 5, 46, 131, 147
reporting, 127, 140
sex after, difficulty of, 144
statistics, 1, 2, 127, 137
talking way out of, 15-16, 89,
   109-110, 134
trauma and, 141
under-reported crime, 127
victim
   as object, 130
   as substitute, 130

when to fight, 113, 132, 135,
   137
See also Dangerous situations, Rapists, and
   Tactics
Rape Crisis Center, 144
"Rape Crisis Syndrome," 142
Rapists, 11, 12, 88, 113, 128,
   131-32, 145
   and dominance, 145
   interviews with, 11, 88, 113
   opportunist, 133
   perverts, 132
   ploys of, 12
   preselecting victims, 128
   psychology of, 128, 131-33,
      145
   psychotics as, 132
   typical, 128
Rappaport, Steward, 7
Ravits, Judy, 78
Rear choke maneuver, 69-71
Record of valuables, 43
Riley, Judge Earl, 7
Robbery, 26, 27, 79, 106-109
   and drug addicts, 107
   foiling, 107, 108
   statistics, 1, 2, 107
Rope jumping, 166
Running (from assailant), 8,
   14-15, 65

S
Safety deposit box, 28
Safety devices for home, 23-27
Screaming, 8, 14-15, 16, 47, 65,
   66, 68, 69, 71, 72, 80, 87
   difficulty, 80
   "fire," 46, 48, 66, 68, 69, 71,
      87
   "help," 47
   practicing, 48
   when not to scream, 48
Sebree, Mrs. Anne, 80

Self-consciousness, 4, 5, 10, 11, 55
Self-defense
  alertness and, 1, 8, 10, 45, 93, 172
  anxiety in learning, 5, 50-51
  against bludgeon, 49, 91
  California law on, 7
  "commensurate with assailant's intention," 7
  delivery, 20-21, 167
  against dog, 97-98
  embarrassment and, 77
  examples of
    See Tactics
  exercises and, 155-72
  failure to learn, 2
  fear in, 112
  five weapons for (bodily), 16-17
  against gun, 89-96
  against knife, 86-88
  legal definition of, 7
  male chauvinism and, 79
  maturity and, 6
  against murder, 111-112
  planning counterattack, 16-17
  practicing, 45, 167-72
  psychological attitudes and, 2, 52
  rage and, 112
  against rape, 54-55, 114, 127-47
    See also Rape, Rapists
  reasons for learning, 65
    inappropriate, 65
  self-consciousness in learning, 4, 5
  shaping-up for, 155-72
  speed in, 20
  against strangling, 69
  tactics, 45-76
  testing knowledge of, 186-90
  when not to attempt, 6

Self Determination (publication), 144
Shock stick, 85
Shoulder strength, exercises for, 157, 158, 162
Side bends, 166
Simonson, Judge Archie, 130
Single-wrist maneuver, 66
Sit-ups, 161
Son of Sam, 132
Speck, Richard, 116
Spine, exercises for, 160
Skyjacking, 37
Stiffness (and exercise), 155
Stomach muscles, exercises for, 161, 162
Straddle stretches, 158-59
Strangling, 69
Strangers, precautions with, 27, 39
Strategy in self-defense, 8
  See also Conroy Method
Streets, safety on, 40-42
  clothing on, 40
  walking with dog, 40
  well-lit, 41
  See also Dangerous situations
Strength, 2, 155
Stretching, 158-59
Stinky (Berkeley rapist), 144-46
Swimming, 166

T
Tactics for self-defense, 8, 45-76
  See also individual tactics
Talking (as tactic), 15-16, 89, 109-110, 134
Target areas, 18-20
  eyes as, 18, 47, 56
  groin as, 18
  knees as, 19
  on men, 18-20
  neck as, 20
  on women, 101

See also Tactics
Tate, Leonard Frank, 147
Taxis
  and rape, 37
  waiting for safety, 37
Tear gas, 77, 85
  delayed reaction to, 77, 78
"Telegraphing," 167
Telephone, precautions with,
  32-34
Test, Kathie, 147
Thumb gouge (eye gouge), 16,
  47, 48-53, 57, 63, 66, 69, 72,
  87, 137
  against assailant wearing
    glasses, 48
  against assailant with gun, 89
  against bludgeon, 49
  blinding assailant, 49
  against choking, 48
  difficult to imagine perform-
    ing, 48, 52
  locating eyes, 53
  practicing, 167, 169, 171
Traveling and safety, 38-39
  planning, 38
  and strangers, 39

U
Umbrella
  as shield, 83
  as spear, 83

V
Vacation, protecting home during, 31-32
Vicious dog, defense against,
  97-98
  fear and, 98
Victim, attitudes of, 10
Victorian attitudes toward
  women's self-defense, 4,
  10

Voice (as defense), 16, 47-48,
  65, 77, 92
  See also Screaming

W
Warning systems, electronic,
  26, 27
Walking, manner of, 10
Weapons, 77-92
  body, 77, 79
  commercially available, 85
  defense against, 86-92
  for defense, 79-80
  false security and, 77
  legality of, 85
  purse, 77
  See also Self-defense
Wells, Alison, 144
Whistle, 80
Windows, bars on, 25
Woman beaters, psychology of,
  98-99
Woman beating, 98-101
  guilt and, 98
  recommendations on, 100
  types of victims, 99
Women
  attacks on, 1
    reporting, 2
    statistics, 1, 2
  gangs, 101
  historical attitudes toward,
    129
  rape and, *See* Rape
  self-defense for, *See* Self-
    defense
  strength of, 2
  Victorian attitudes toward,
    4, 10
  vulnerable areas of, 101
See also Dangerous situations, Rape, Self-defense,
  and Tactics